SLAVERY
CONTINUES

SLAVERY CONTINUES

HOPE OF BREAKING THE CHAINS

Mehr A. Kalami

iUniverse LLC
Bloomington

SLAVERY CONTINUES
HOPE OF BREAKING THE CHAINS

iUniverse books may be ordered through booksellers or by contacting:

iUniverse LLC
1663 Liberty Drive
Bloomington, IN 47403
www.iuniverse.com
1-800-Authors (1-800-288-4677)

ISBN: 978-1-4917-3381-3 (sc)
ISBN: 978-1-4917-3382-0 (e)

Library of Congress Control Number: 2014908111

Printed in the United States of America.

iUniverse rev. date: 05/05/2014

CONTENTS

Historically, the most terrible things-war, genocide and slavery-have resulted not from disobedience, but from obedience.

Howard Zinn

DEDICATION

This work is dedicated to those innocent and sinless human beings who lost their precious lives at the hands of slave owners and their agents, professional enslavers whom we identify as despots, tyrants and vicious beings; masquerading as leaders, politicians, individual human beings, priests, preachers and clergymen through the ages.

Let this be a somber reminder of remembrance for those human beings whose brief lives were snatched from them by people wielding dominance over their very existence; enslavers.

Let us in all honesty remember this vastitude of enslaved human beings whose numbers exceed a billion people during the millenniums; those people who were enslaved so that a few could live in opulence and luxury. From more than five million people of African origin, many of whom died while in transit to slavery, to a similar figure of gallant and brave Native Indians of the American Continent who were ruthlessly massacred for no reason to the countless Aborigines in Australia who were murdered by settlers just for the joy of killing another human being!

A special salute to the innocent millions whose precious lives were snuffed out in specially designed crematoriums in death and labor camps, by cheering and jeering enslaved cowards dressed as soldiers, nurses and so-called doctors who called themselves protectors of the State, by obeying orders from a mentally depraved dictator. The victims' only fault was not to be a Gentile!

A moment of remembrance for those numbering more than a hundred million human beings presently held in various forms of slavery, bondage and incarceration in medieval style dungeons at the orders of fanatic dictators. Whether in the garb of a Muslim clergyman, a Christian priest, a Buddhist monk or an individual dressed in a three-piece suit or in the honorable uniform of a soldier, the despot is an ultimate in crime.

Then comes the case of nearly half a million "invisible" slaves in Iran under a Theocratic regime; the Baha'is, who are prevented from obtaining education, from practicing their faith, from travelling and leaving the country and even banned and barred from the bare necessities of life; access to medical aid.

One must in all honesty agree that an unbiased study will prove that the victims of slavery then and now are in an unimaginable situation; worse than the combined effects of the Justinian and the Black Plague and the Influenza Pandemic, that struck the lives of tens of millions of beings throughout the world. If the plagues and the pandemics were noted and "seen," and finally felt, the pernicious "plague of slavery" is invisible, but deadlier since it appears incurable and continuous; at least for the present times.

In every literary work that I have penned, words of dedication are always there; to those who have relevance to my work. In this work, I have to remember those closest to me, those who have played an amicable role in my struggles in life, friends, whose presence and past will eternally be a part of my life.

Near and dear ones whose lives meant and means very much to me; Danielle Uttama Kreis, my honored friend; writer and author who unceasingly fought injustice and human dominance and who entered the spirit stage in August 9, 2011 in Geneva, Switzerland.

Holistic expert, writer and author Anouchka Von Heuer who has championed the cause of the forgotten and the downtrodden who encouraged me to pen this work. On October 5, 2001, under the patronage of the President of France, and the French Foreign Minister, the Government of France decorated Ms. Von Heuer with the Silver and Gold medals for her contributions to French Culture and Literature. I feel obliged to remember Mrs. Inga Stauffer-Heuer, who selflessly dedicated a larger part of her life to the needs of the homeless and poor, especially those forced to flee their homelands for a variety of reasons. In addition, a host of others who have helped me, encouraged me, and even "resuscitated" me. I acknowledge them. I honor them.

Allow me to list some of the few heroes bravely acting to put an end to modern-day slavery in each and every form with selfless devotion and courage.

Angelina Atyam, co-founder of Concerned Parents' Association, Uganda. Nancy Kassebaum, former U.S. Senator and longtime activist against human trafficking. Jacqueline Thibault, President-Founder, *Fondation Surgir*, (The Arise Foundation), Lausanne, Switzerland. Ansar Burney, Chairman, Ansar Burney Welfare Trust International, Pakistan. Amod Kanth, Inspector General of Police, Indian Police Service and founder of NGO "Prayas;" New Delhi, India. Somaly Mam and Pierre Legros, co-founders, "Acting for At-Risk Women (*Agir pour Les Femmes En Situation Precaire-AFESIP*), Southeast Asia. The daring Journalist Adiba Umarova from the Republic of Tajikistan, who investigated trafficking of human beings from Tajikistan to several West European countries and Sheikhdoms. Almost all those trafficked finally ended up as slaves. Albeit imminent dangers to her own life, she followed and hunted down the criminals and exposed them to the United Nations and other related World Organizations. Photographer and filmmaker Mimi Chakarova, recipient of the Nestor Almendros Award for her filmmaking at the Human Rights Film Festival in New York and for her untiring war against trafficking and enslavement. The globally honored Anuradha Koirala, one of the founders of "Maiti Nepal" in 1993, which is the most active foundation, helping to resuscitate thousands of lives destroyed by sex-slavery, trafficking and forced labor in Nepal. Koirala, through her selfless efforts helped rescue and even rehabilitate more than twelve thousand women and young girls from a life of enslaved prostitution and various forms of bondage.

Allow me to remember Mira Sorvino, Oscar-winning actress and good will ambassador to combat human trafficking for the U.N. Office on Drugs and Crime, which tackles human trafficking

To the late icon of Indian movies, Feroz Khan (1939-2009), who was one of the founders of the several societies in India actively seeking to arrest and bring to justice traffickers and agents of slavery. To other film stars of India, prominent among them Anil Kapoor and Akshay Kumar, Paresh Rawal, Katrina Kaif, Vishwanath "Nana" Patekar and Malika Sherawat who have devoted their lives to gallantly fight slavery in India and elsewhere in the world.

To Her Majesty Queen Silvia of Sweden who for the past several years has been vigorously leading an untiring campaign in fighting child sex trafficking and slavery.

To His Majesty King Juan Carlos Alfonso Victor Maria de Borbon y Borbon-Dos Sicilias of Spain for his continued protection of the minorities in Spain.

To the globally decorated and renowned Professor and writer, Jean Ziegler, the relentless champion of Human Rights and a former member of the Advisory Committee of the United Nations Human Rights Council. The professor, always with the lesser privileged, made history when he awakened the conscience of the world with a short sentence when he said, "A child who dies from hunger is a murdered child."

Ziegler, a well-known humanist, in his latest writings titled: "*Destruction massive—Geopolitique de la faim*" (Mass Destruction—the Geopolitics of Hunger) argues that no human being should go hungry and that the world could well feed nearly twelve billion people. That could be a direct reference to State-sponsored slavery where the enslaved who are subjected to forced labor could be fed rather than allowed to die due to hunger, or that part of the world, where hunger and malnourishment kills hundreds of thousands each year, while there is plenty of food for all, that could be delivered to them from other parts of the world.

A word of honor to Dewa Hughese, popular Media Celebrity, Women's Empowerment Minister of Indonesia and Indonesia's ambassador and spokesperson for the Campaign to Eliminate Trafficking in Women and Children. The popular Ricky Martin, founder of Ricky Martin Foundation who has devoted his time and resources to improving the lives of children around the world. Aida Mbodj of Senegal; who has taken a strong stand against exploitative child begging in Senegal and finally "Sisters of

Adoration, Slaves of the Blessed Sacrament and of Charity, Lima, Peru" who have been providing medical attention to trafficking victims.

I feel persuaded to remember Rabbi Harold Kushner of Temple Israel of Natick, a supporter of justice and goodwill towards humanity and the immortal fountain of sagacity, Osho "who never lived and never died." Osho's writings and lectures always touched the absolute equality of humankind with no individual having any form of superiority over others.

Ere it be late, allow me to hasten to also dedicate this work to His Majesty King Abdulla II of the Hashemite Kingdom of Jordan for being one of the most benign statesman since the past century; a person with very special convictions with the least tolerance for any form of slavery in the Kingdom. Both the King and Queen Rania have vigorously pursued Human Rights and the evils of slavery throughout the world.

Her Majesty, Farah Pahlavi, the former Empress of Iran who has and continues to dedicatedly help prevent prostitution and related miseries which have often led to slavery to young Iranian girls and women who have escaped the Islamic regime in Tehran. It is not a hypothesis, but an undeniable truth, that without the former Empress' untiring dedication to humanity, thousands of precious lives would have been wasted through the evils of child prostitution, forced labor and outright slavery.

Let me also dedicate this work to heroic men and women throughout the world who have repeatedly stood up courageously against the evils of slavery with some of them paying the ultimate price for supporting this noble cause. There are such unsung heroes in the USA, Russia, France, Switzerland, Norway, Iran, The Netherlands, Denmark, Norway, Sweden, Pakistan and India and in several Baltic and the Balkan States.

Finally, a special word of thanks to F. A. Rahimi for contributing to the computer effects of this literary work.

Mehr A. Kalami
Former Political Attaché at the Permanent Mission of
Iran to the United Nations, Geneva, Switzerland

INTRODUCTION

"The Moving Finger writes; and having writ,
Moves on: nor all thy Piety nor Wit,
Shall lure it back to cancel half a Line,
Nor all thy Tears wash out a Word of it."

Omar Khayyam

"There is no form of benign slavery! There was no such thing.
It is slavery, pure and simple. It is mankind versus mankind!
However you look at it, it is slavery." Author

For the past several years, perhaps as long as a decade ago, I have been preparing my thoughts to more profoundly investigate the murky world of slavery and the horrors that accompany it. Horrors that are beyond the imagination and concept of the common mind. Horrors that are prescribed for humankind by humankind! Horrors that are manifested in all its misery. Horrors that are administered to mankind-by-mankind which in finality spell slavery leading to his or her premature demise through the power of suggestion and on the promise of a better life.

The power of suggestion, obfuscation, lies, deceit and promises are utilized by those human beings laying pretence to the role of a guide, a helper, a master, a leader, a succor and a redeemer of humanity! Those imposters are the individuals who finally turn out to be their victim's sorrows, pains, chains, fetters and finally enslavement until the unfortunate victims die or are killed and disposed off as a "waste" matter unfit to live.

Political changes have had with it results for the worse since it is crystal clear that the politician was never and is never there for the general public. He is for himself and his own vested interest. Whether a Monarch, a

President, a Prime Minister, a Dictator, a leader or even someone fairly and officially elected to office, he cares the least! Mankind is left to himself to trudge in life and to find a way out of this quagmire made for him by other human beings. That was a part of arcane "geo-politics" and I had vowed to explore some part of it; that part which dealt with the enslavement of human beings by none but our fellow human beings.

I am a researcher and a writer, and an ordinary voice from the crowd, the teeming millions who also want to make a statement, a statement to clear their consciences by speaking out their minds.

Considering the subject matter of my work, I feel obliged to repeat several statements to refresh my readers' thoughts on this very contested subject.

In my case, I have to handle this episode alone. There are no persons to be thanked and considered as those who either encouraged me or suggested the subject matter of this work. Cosmology, and not eschatology in the least, has always played a salient role in my literary works.

In presenting my thoughts, I have no intention to appease, glorify or denounce any individual. The facts are documented and verifiable. No attempts are made to present this work as a work full of thrill, excitement and drama or to advocate misguidance by falsifying or exaggerating statistics and figures about those human beings who were relieved of their most precious thing on earth; their lives, by fellow human beings.

Enslavement of mankind-by-mankind is the supreme evil, thought and enacted by human beings, ostensibly to tear apart the very fabric of society into the rule and the ruled, those that govern and those that are governed. There is no status and strata in between.

Chains, fetters and ball that include with it forced labor are not the only factors to determine the enslaved. Sexual exploitation is nothing less, if not, the worst. Trafficking, abducting and kidnapping human beings are yet other forms of slavery.

There is no lowest form of slavery! All and any type of slavery is just low! To enslave and dominate is not heroism. It is cowardice at its lowest tide, since it calls for the dominance of the strong on the feeble and the rich on the poor. The have-nots are at the mercy of the haves.

The United Nations has prepared a list of definitions which it insists are the sources of identification as to whether a human being is in reality enslaved or not, or whether the known and recognized assault of mankind on mankind really adds up to the evils of slavery.

An observation into this not so dark and murky subject, wherein there should be a research as to if a life first enchained and then destroyed by another human, could be after all, identified as leading to slavery or not, is indeed facile. This is not the subject of solving mathematical equations. It is easily felt and understood. There is wealth to be made. There is income to be had in this vile trade. This is the intentional destruction of one life to benefit from. This is the planned elimination of a human being by reducing him to an object and stripping him of his dignity and honor. This is slavery! People and Societies crumble while a few unscrupulous lives richen on the bones, blood and flesh of the fallen, the forgotten and the damned. An end to a life comes as soon as slavery commences. The end result is death with misery.

Common sense dictates that simple thinking and reasons within the common mind would identify enslavement to be synonymous with the following deeds:

Enslavement equals to sex trade where a human body is up for sale as if it is private property of the prophesied "owner." It is also identifiable with sex trafficking and recruiting, harboring, transporting or obtaining a person for forced labor to involuntary servitude and commercial sex act.

Enslavement also equals debt bondage, coercion, slave labor and anything that could hamper or jeopardize any individual human being's capacity and ability to think, write, travel and believe in any faith.

Enslavement is nothing less to forcing political prisoners to toil in the heat and the cold sixteen to eighteen hours a day, beaten for the slightest infringement, and left to die of malnourishment or if ailing from any disease or injury due to a new lifestyle imposed on him or her by his "political-owners."

Enslavement is also the same as throwing political opponents into primitive and medieval dungeons and leaving them to starve to death by invoking divine teachings as justifications.

Enslavement also equals to beating, imprisoning and even murdering personal opponents by making it appear because of high treason or sedition against the State. The worst accusation is "waging a war against god" in a theocratic regime.

Enslavement also equals to preventing, controlling, limiting movements, barring the practice of any faith, belief and religion.

It is interesting to examine the amiable "prescription" created by the United Nations for the enslaver and the enslaved. It needs no elaboration! It is an affront to humanity.

The definitions determined by the United Nations as to who are the offenders and who are the offended and turned into a guideline is a pleasant reminder to the victimizer that he is not considered as a criminal, a murderer, an individual deserving the highest degree of punishment by any court of laws in any country in any continent. In face, none of the "guidelines to identify the enslaver" as presented by the United Nations has any significance or effect.

Below are the exact statements of the United Nation's definition, which create more questions that it could answer about the purpose of this page.

Definition of "Severe Forms of Trafficking in Persons" VERE FORMS OF TRAFFICKING IN PERSONS"

The Trafficking Victims Protection Act dated 2005 defines "severe form of trafficking in persons" as

(a) **sex trafficking** in which a **commercial sex act** is induced by force, fraud, or **coercion**, or in which the person induced to perform such an act has not attained 18 years of age; or

(b) the recruitment, harboring, transportation, provision, or obtaining of a person for labor or services, through the use of force, fraud, or **coercion** for the purpose of subjection to **involuntary servitude**, peonage, **debt bondage**, or slavery.

Definition of Terms Used in the Term "Severe Forms of Trafficking in Persons"

"Sex trafficking" means the recruitment, harboring, transportation, provision, or obtaining of a person for the purpose of a commercial sex act.

"Commercial sex act" means any sex act on account of which anything of value is given to or received by any person.

"Involuntary servitude" includes a condition of servitude induced by means of (a) any scheme, plan, or pattern intended to cause a person to believe that, if the person did not enter into or continue in such condition, that person or another person would suffer serious harm or physical restraint; or (b) the abuse or threatened abuse of the legal process.

"Debt bondage" means the status or condition of a debtor arising from a pledge by the debtor of his or her personal services or of those of a person under his or her control as a security for debt, if the value of those services as reasonably assessed is not applied toward the liquidation of the debt or the length and nature of those services are not respectively limited and defined.

"Coercion" means (a) threats of serious harm to or physical restraint against any person; (b) any scheme, plan or pattern intended to cause a person to believe that failure to perform an act would result in serious harm to or physical restraint against any person; or, (c) the abuse or threatened abuse of the legal process.

No standard form of punishment can ever be determined for infringements in case of any individual country, since every country has its own laws. Unless and until this scourge could be categorized as a global infraction, then only a standard form of punishment could be prescribed.

A most recent conspicuous example of criminals going unpunished or "sentenced" with a simple admonishment is that of Wolfgang Schwarz, the former Austrian skating champion.

The Associated Press on August 7, 2006 reported that Schwarz, who was deeply involved in the sex-slave trade for several years, was arrested, tried and convicted in Vienna. His arrest came only after the relatives of the victims and the Anti Slavery International with the Austrian Justice system lodged more than a hundred complaints.

Wolfgang Schwarz headed a gang of traffickers who kidnapped and smuggled underage girls from Lithuania, Russia, Ukraine, Romania and Bulgaria into Austria for the pleasure of rich tycoons, usually German nationals who owned expensive chalets in various parts of south Austria. An unrepentant Schwarz participated in the virtual destruction of more than two thousand lives!

He was tried and given a sentence of eight years but finally sentenced to eighteen months! This sentence too was postponed since the judge was informed that Schwarz was unwell due to the side effects of medical treatment. As of March 2014, he has not served a day in prison. In monologues in the streets of Vienna, he claimed he had helped the society in putting food on the table of the parents of poor girls with no hope in life. An investigation by Anti Slavery International proved that none of the parents of the thousands of victims knew of the whereabouts of their missing children.

After his trial and on being freed, Schwarz often dressed as a Catholic preacher in public claiming that god had personally spoken to him and blessed him several times while his trial was underway.

Reports by several watchdog societies in Austria involved in covertly investigating slavery stated that Schwarz had attempted suicide, at least on three occasions.

Other factors such as proving the severity of the deed, the number of slaves, their treatment or the degree of atrocities inflicted on them are a hindrance. The traffickers, agents and above them, the slave dealers, know fully well that this would be a very difficult procedure for the law and hence their total free hand in doing and acting as they please.

Such a picture would only serve to relay the message of protection for the criminals and their agents with no form of protection for the victims.

A FEW WORDS WITH
THE READER

"Conceit may puff a man up,
But can never prop him up."

John Ruskin

In preparing this work, I have labored to present the undeniable truth, as harsh and as gruesome as it may appear. I lay no claims to any academic pretensions or to any special aura of wisdom. I am just another person taking the opportunity to relay a simple message to the reader; a message to search within one self the reasons as to why humanity has allowed slavery in so many forms and all its ills to go untamed and uncontrolled during the past tens of thousands of years. Most important of all, the goals in this work are to urge the common person to think and plan effective ways and means to smash the chains and fetters of bondage and slavery, forever.

I ask the reader to patiently comprehend the several reasons behind my statements, some of them thought provoking and virtually challenging them, both directly and indirectly to openly speak their mind and make their beliefs manifested with courage against those who supposedly claim to be their trusted representatives of constituencies in the political organizations of their home country. Of paramount importance is the need to relay the message to mount a real war against those human beings and those elements in this world who consider themselves as the anointed ones to enslave others. To persuade their politician-representatives to arise from their deep stupor and to aggressively call on the other governments of the world to step up their efforts against this disease, even if it means to fight slavery on a war footing if every peaceful means fail.

Mankind is strange; their manners strange; their moods strange, their beliefs strange to a certain extent, their philosophies strange and stranger yet is their inner feelings to dominate; to dominate their own kin, humanity in general.

Since ancient times, the criminal mind existed and they exist today. Since times immemorial, the adventure-seeking conqueror existed and many of them still exist in one form or the other. Such beings do not carry a tag and a label informing us of their nefarious and notorious plans or their plan of action. None, not even a single person around them; even those considered their inner-circle are unaware what the tyrant wants and what are his next moves.

A conqueror who has murdered his way into another country is not only cheered, he is also hailed as a "liberator;" by the nation whom he has just conquered. Paean of praise and slogans embellish him as their savior and invest him with a halo of super human glory at regular intervals, albeit his heritage is dubious and his goals questionable. To the eyes of the unaware, he becomes a liberator, a hero, a champion to their cause. He regularly laments what he imagines to be the torments the people had to undergo by their former ruler. His power of suggestion is successful and the people obfuscated. They believe in his falsity. Less than a day later, the so-called liberated people are imprisoned en-masse and condemned to die a sure death at the hands of their "liberator!"

History has proved to us these developments wherein a blood-thirsty dictator becomes the liberator of the supposedly enslaved, the so-called oppressed and the under-privileged but sooner or later, under a pretext or the other, creates death, destruction, bloodshed and misery throughout that country, he supposedly has liberated.

Not too long in the past, such things happened in Russia with the Bolsheviks entering the scene as the champions of the masses. Nearly a hundred million Russians lost their precious lives to these goons masquerading as their liberators in less than eight decades. The Russians were enslaved by the tens of millions, making them the largest concentration of slaves in any part of the world at any time in recorded history. It was a "joint" form of dictatorship to enslave one and all without blame being leveled on any single individual. The ruling hierarchy was the unclearly defined Supreme Soviet, the snake pit of skullduggery and enslavement of the general population. Millions were simply murdered in cold blood by these "liberators!"

The same approach of lying and deceit took place in Ethiopia where radicals dethroned the King and where the nation is still reeling in misery and backwardness. It happened in Afghanistan when the King was toppled and where death and misery continues until today.

It did happen in Iran in 1979 where the King was first destabilized by foreign powers and ousted to pave the way for a sacerdotal regime under an unknown and a virtually illiterate clergyman then, and his successor; an equally illiterate preacher now who has claimed the mantle of a leader; the type of which history has never witnessed. There, even in recent days, several people, often in dozens, are executed once every few weeks throughout the country at a given time, while the succeeding clergyman leader warmly smiles to the still dazed and frightened nation.

Shocking and unbelievable, but true, an ethnic minority of "seyeds," a non-Iranian people of Arab origin constituting a mere 3 percent of the 76 million people have enslaved the majority Indo-European Iranian people! The people wanted "freedom" and the wily clergymen were there to cater to their needs.

It happened in Germany, in Italy, in Spain, in Ethiopia, in Chile, in Argentina, in Liberia, in Egypt, in Libya, in China and elsewhere where dictators betrayed the trust of the people and instead put them in perpetual misery or dragged them to their death through wars!

Of special significance is Germany where a mentally unstable non-German, not only laid out the plans for the systematic murder of more than seven million people whom he considered to be as "non-Gentile", but that he also destroyed a country and its people which had no relation to him ethnically or otherwise. The enslaver vainly tried to identify himself with the Deutsch speaking people of Germany. The German citizenry saw in him a perfect example of an enslaver but were powerless. His war mongering tactics and cruelties ignited a World War resulting in the death of more than fifty million men, women and children throughout the world. The enslaver-dictator thus achieved such a terrible crime of this magnitude during his twelve years and a few months in power through sheer mind-enslavement. His end came as expected, violently, through his own blood-soaked hands with less than a hundred people around him.

Enslavers are everywhere and in every form possible. In Syria, the al Assad regime continues to orchestrate a blood bath while smiling to the lens of the foreign news media.

It happened in Iraq decades ago when the King was murdered to usher in a state of horror and virtual enslavement for at least four and half decades. Saddam Hussein Tekriti was the result of this revolution. The USA took the bold initiative to further stop one of the cruelest regimes in modern history in Iraq. However, the people still suffer; and it continues until today even with the dictator executed. History has proved that a dictator is there not to safeguard the interest of the country he pretends to administer, but to protect his own existence.

What if the reader is asked a simple question; as to what would be the inner feelings of a sane individual to see a human being in slavery, bondage and fetters whose identity has been changed, whose diet has been changed, his religious beliefs and clothing changed? In short, his very existence has been changed totally to suit the pride, ego and an evil philosophy of his owner!

In present day authoritarian regimes, most of the dictators are puppets of other powers, however vehemently they may deny it. Whether the West or Eastern Powers have poured and continued to pour oil into the lamps of these "mass-enslavers" is not important, most important is how to oust them and put an end to the life of slavery, which they have inflicted on the common people whom they have supposedly liberated!

What is common in a totalitarian government is that all ruling heads have a surreptitious agenda; enslavement, death, bloodshed, destruction and imprisonment for the people they supposedly administer. A simple glimpse into such horrifying rules continually reminds us is that it is always the minority that rules the majority!

Rarely does the unpopular strongman venture out of his stronghold for a stroll or an outing. He stays within the confines of his own "fortress;" a prisoner of his own making, a prisoner unto himself. He too is a prisoner like the nation he has imprisoned. Has any dictator been ever glorified as a benevolent despot, a benign enslaver, a spiritual murderer?

Determination and an Iron Will is the only way to remedy this evil! Slavery will remain until the day the governments are kept apart by heads of regimes that refuse to join hands with benign governments to oust this menace for the last time. Uncouth regimes benefit from slavery, since for them it is a way to control and check the nation. The head of the unpopular regime is in fact the "enslaver-in-chief" of the nation he supposedly administers.

The individual despot is a common human being with the same physiognomy and physical description except for his regal attire and paid soothsayers and agitators around him, which magnifies him as an intimidating and an imposing totem pole to the public. The enslaver-ruler is reduced to a pile of invisible ashes if the masses for once decidedly and courageously tell him, "No more!" He will evaporate in a moment. He will disappear and vanish, just as he came. He may be able to escape, but will be caught, arrested and his false scaffolding dismantled.

We have all witnessed the ends of dictators; almost all of them were alone in their final days. Their presence in Germany, Iraq, Italy, Chile, Congo, Argentina, Egypt, Liberia, Libya, Ethiopia, Uganda and the Islamic regime in Tehran are some examples in recent years. Often is the case where the enslaver is overtly hailed and praised but passionately detested from within the minds of the common public.

CHAPTER I

THE HORROR

"Machine men, with machine minds and machine hearts!
You are not machines, you are not cattle, you are men! You
have the love of humanity in your hearts. You don't hate: only
the unloved hate, the unloved and the unnatural. Soldiers,
don't fight for slavery, fight for liberty! You the people have
the power, the power to create machines, the power to create
happiness! You the people have the power to make this life free
and beautiful, to make this life a wonderful adventure! Then,
in the name of democracy, let us use that power. Let us all
unite! Let us fight for a new world, a decent world."

Charles Chaplin

Has any single individual wearing a costly and designer sweater with
a three piece-suit and scarf with expensive kerchief and fancy socks or
dresses and stockings, ever pondered for a short moment as to from which
textile mills the fabric was produced and later turned into a finished
product for him? Imagine the same with his children! Has that individual
ever thought of knowing the several procedures that went to make what
he or she is wearing and brandishing as a sign of opulence, wealth and
luxury? Finally, have those individuals garbed in designer suits and
dresses ever cared to know who were the unfortunate people that helped
make them appear attractive through such outfits? Whom were the
damned and those considered as the condemned who assisted in adding
charm to their appearance?

In the same vein, has the financially well off individual throwing a
sumptuous party at his opulent mansion serving a variety of shrimp;

small, medium, large, extra-large and jumbo together with a variety of fish raised in large man-made ponds ever cared to think that they are from fish-farms who have been employing slave-labor for decades and more?

Consider that he is feasting on special cuts of beef with his guests while not caring to know that the cattle were cared and raised by forced labor! Has any person shown an iota of interest about the origins of those fine fresh vegetables flown in from Central and South America or from Central Asia with lots of words of praise on their labels or how the fragrant flowers attractively arranged on the tables have been grown or raised?

Unfortunately, the rich and the chosen ones have never cared to investigate the source and the means of production of the items they feast upon with their equally elegant-appearing affluent guests or the products they purchase to augment their luxurious life-style.

Mankind placing mankind in chains and fetters. A matter of one human being holding another human being in bondage in this very century; the twenty first century! It is unbelievable and shocking by all means. That also, in countries and societies, which claim advancement in science and technology?

Countless centuries of research, discussions, round-tables, lectures, symposiums and exchange of opinions by Sociologists, Psychologists, Holistic experts, Politicians and Historians have only been able to reflect the ills and effects of this evil without suggesting any real remedy. Slavery is alive and well! The officious head of this ultimate evil hangs over the lives of the forgotten, the downtrodden and the under privileged like an ominous phantom.

From the very moment we are born, the ominous signs of rule over us never cease to leave us until our last breath! Being enslaved in one way or the other has now become a part of humanity's life and living.

The word "Slavery" needs no elaboration! It is self-explanatory. To clarify it and to remove any ambiguity, just a few concise explanations suffice for this torturous word. "The state of one bound in servitude as the property of a slaveholder or household," and "The practice of owning slaves," or simply: "The subjection of one person to another person, especially in being forced to work for the benefit of the enslaver." Were ever a topic of Slavery be written, hundreds of volumes and pages after pages of definitions defining the enslaved would be insufficient!

The global community still wonders in awe and disbelief as to why after all with the several hundreds of Declarations and Resolutions prohibiting, condemning human bondage and defining and using human beings as chattels, the scourge continues and continues unabated and often with a stronger vigor in one form or the other.

"Freedom of Mankind" appears to be a topic, perhaps only enjoyed to be "further discussed and examined" by several International Organizations and Societies but no concrete steps has ever been taken to create a "roving watchdog" to monitor this trade with a sworn determination. Such a document does not exist! Verbally it may have been discussed but it ends there and then. Slavery continues unbridled with greater fervor. One may ask as to why should the global community discuss or care about humankind's captivity and bondage brought about by none other than humanity itself, the unbridled exploitation and enslavement of one human being by another.

The United Nations can only pass a few resolutions, declarations and some more feeble official admonishments and even pleas to the ruling heads or hierarchies of regimes suspected of enslaving their nation. No response is ever demanded of the offending regime or governments. Beyond this, there are no concrete steps nor any standardized procedure or an acceptable and workable mechanism to monitor this vile deed and to put an end to this diabolic trade.

The Various International Organizations are too loath to sacrifice and jeopardize their financial situations by confronting any defaulting government. Human bondage is in many forms and kinds, and all deal with the lives of human beings! In virtually every country of the world at any given time, there is slavery and such an abominable deed thrives and even goes untamed.

Since the last twenty-five centuries and more, slavery has been given a boost due to wars, skirmishes and conflicts. Even before that, quarrels, fights, invasion of one another's properties ended in some form of domination by a group against another, one clan against another, one family on another! War's results were not only to be treasures and land; it also included human beings, human beings to slave and labor for the winner. The imprisoned and enchained and the vanquished lived, while being dead, and died while still alive.

Even the victors were slaves to their own philosophies in life. Their leaders and commanders were slaves to higher echelons in their hierarchy. They too were slaves!

Democracy is a theory; there are no standards and sets of rule to democracy. It is a figment of the mind, an imagination! Nevertheless, the people can contest and even protest wrongdoings to the point of challenging the government. Whereas in a Sacerdotal form of government, massive and violent punishments and torments are inflicted upon those who dare challenge the government or the clergyman who rules by decree, often citing religious edicts and codes as the reason.

In truth, the tyrant leading a theocratic government does everything possible to stay in power. His nefarious deeds prove that he is not divinely inspired. His desires and greed for power encourage him to enslave. In fact, he is the paragon of evil. He legalizes and passes them as canonic laws. Almost all such acts are by the Muslim clergyman and in a few cases a Christian preacher. In order to punish the captive of his misdeeds and his despotism, shackles, chains, whippings, tortures of every type are permissible! Death by execution is simply the finality of the religious despot's orders. This is slavery.

This is not the micro presentation of slavery. This social plague has no frontiers and its date of commencement is shrouded in mystery. If forced servitude and forced-prostitution is a form of slavery that we are witnessing today, then one must bore deeper into the more ghoulish form of slavery; fettered and enchained with a ball! It could be easily perceived as to how horrifying that could have been.

Sociologists and Academics from Switzerland, Iran, France, Germany and the Subcontinent even believe that this tragedy is destined to continue in one form or the other for thousands of years to come! Perhaps millions of years ago when the first man walking on two evolved around a society, there was a form of struggle to maintain a hierarchy and hence the rest were dominated, a form of beginnings to this evil. Nevertheless, there are men and women of courage who still struggle to cap this sinister philosophy and way of life with a ray of hope for the future.

In case the theory or concept of slavery has to be expanded and extended, the act of brainwashing, mind molesting and manipulations by the Christian preacher, the guru, the master and the Muslim clergyman unfailingly add up to a form of enslavement.

The individual guru, master, preacher and clergyman have steps to follow to achieve their goals. He has to first influence the audience to believe in him, have faith in whatever he says by injecting in them fervor, hysteria and mass hallucination as to what has to be performed by them in order to satisfy god or the Cosmos. This is the commencement of mental enslavement. Mental enslavement can be definitely related to a form of slavery since the subject will do anything he has been asked to do by the self-appointed attorney and representative of god and spiritual forces on earth, even to the extent of a barbaric and a murderous act.

There are no boundaries to the ultimate in evil. There is no limit to prove their superiority over other human beings. The faithful in any religious center or those listening to a sermon by a master or a guru are virtually hypnotized in not only listening to him but also passively accepting whatever flows from the speaker's mouth. This is a form of "willing slavery" where the common human being volunteers to be a slave, for no reason or objective or even for the betterment of his own life, but just to feel fine that he is a follower.

Strange but true, such individuals pride themselves to become slaves of a self-styled teacher, guru, master, leader and dutifully obey any form of claims by the orator whose only motive is to lay invisible mastery on his crowd.

Many, indeed thousands today lay claim to be the guardians of other human beings in one form or the other. Claims to be the chosen one or anointed by god to tend the flock are but a few. More appropriately, one may conclude, "Slavery by the people, of the people and for the people."

It is a fact that the topic of slavery can never be considered as a scholarly study but attempts can be made to unravel the mysteries that create what is "Modern-Day Slavery."

Can slavery be defined in a strict form or manner? Can it ever be narrowed down to the concept of putting a human being in fetters and chains and forcing him and her to labor and die while laboring? Is any form of research or symposium required to identify the arcane features and definitions that can rightfully be categorized as slavery? The question is so simple and the answer appears as simple. There is no need to research and to hold any symposium. Slavery is Slavery!

There are dozens, perhaps hundreds of forms of slavery! However, the more conspicuous ones appear to be a few ones: mental, physical, social, economic, labor, psychological and through the factors of Colonialism, Imperialism, Communism, Capitalism and Theocracy. Much has been spoken and written about Democracy. No sooner than one defends his rights to speak and defend his very existence as a part of "Democracy" then the words "Republic" eclipses his every words.

In the USA, as soon as any individual claims his inalienable right to reflect his thoughts, he is accused of being an anarchist with the ubiquitous words; "The USA is not a Democracy, it is a Republic!" In addition, statements like; "it is most anti-American to do so and think so." You would be shouted down with the words; "Which and what form of freedom is further required? The Republic has everything."

All of these gangs in the garb of members of Political Groups and Organizations finally have one goal; to subjugate, to enchain, to imprison, to eliminate and most important of all to bring about the absolute enslavement of the individual, the society, the people or the nation in its entirety! Included in this vile circle of slavery, are embedded the evil of all evils: trafficking children, child prostitution and child labor which translates into abyssal slavery itself.

There is no natural force creating the slave and the enslaver. The enslaved are in fact the enablers of the enslaver! The enslaver and the enslaved are not different from us in most ways. They are just human beings, our own kin. The enslaved nation in the present tense is that very same nation who in the past tense cheered and hailed the enslaver as a liberator and as a succourer of humankind.

Moreover, he, if a clergyman or priest, usually claims to communicate with god and to receive divine inspiration for each of his later acts whether vicious, vile or nefarious. An invisible ball and chain are generously placed onto the lives of the general public by the enslaver as a divine will, the reasons of which he only knows.

The clergyman despot usually has a state-sponsored audience with a floor director who in fact orchestrates the public who hail and praise the tyrant at given intervals thus impressing the nation who stand by in utter silence. He is the ultimate in mind manipulation. He is the confident trickster and the master of oration and mass-hysteria. He promises every form of comfort for the masses and once comfortably seated in the chair of power, betrays the very same people whom he tricked into hailing him as their undisputed leader. He justifies all his acts against the people as the wish of god.

Of priests and preachers, Suzan B. Anthony said: "I distrust those people who know so well what God wants to do, because I notice it always coincides with their own desires."

Of invoking heaven and hell, Professor Stephen Hawking, world famed physicist and mathematician on May 15, 2011, said: "A belief that heaven or an afterlife awaits us is a 'fairy story' for people afraid of death."

Thugs surrounding the clergyman play the role of the common citizen singing odes of praise to the clergy-enslaver-autocrat who feels further empowered to torment the public in the name of god. Mankind aiding each other to subjugate the masses for a reward in the afterlife.

The military or civilian dictator on the other hand has the government employees, kept in perpetual need, and the paid militia in civilian clothing to comprise their crowd. He too, like the clergyman, directs the orchestra of mass-hysteria and mind-molestation, laced with threats.

The clergyman ruler while issuing threats; particularly god's wrath if he is disobeyed, specializes in falsehood, lies, manipulation, obfuscation, deceit, self-praise, quotation of false events, speaks on the special moments of his direct communications with the Omniscient One and lectures both pleadingly as well as threateningly.

The civilian oppressor continues to speak about ways and means to bring about order in the land through his methods and philosophies, which he claims is for the betterment of the State and the people.

It would be of subtle interest to note that the majority of those heading a theocracy are devoid of any academic education while some are virtually illiterate and ignorant of world events but well schooled in the art of controlling the public. To them, academic education and any form of knowledge dealing with Arts and Science are undesired in the eyes of the Creator.

Blemished and falsified "eschatology" forms the very core of the lifeline of these individuals who mock and eschew superstitious beliefs in private while they preach it to the ever-obedient nation they supposedly administer! Lying, deceit and the total falsification of events and history are their specialty while embellishing themselves and their deeds as an act and will of destiny.

Authoritarian governments rarely judge dissenters, but condemn them as purveyors of decadence, sedition, agents of foreign powers and reactionaries. Many are either sent to the gallows or face a firing squad. The presiding judges are mere pawns and tools in the hands of the ruling hierarchy who draw blood in whichever way they can.

In present day China, labels of foreign spy or stooge of Imperialism is a choice accusation. Of interest is that the non-clergy dictators may have had some educational background, Napoleon Bonaparte, Augusto

Pinochet, Lenin, Stalin, Mao, and Mussolini to name a few of the tyrannical enslavers.

One may have heard or read about Nero, Genghis Khan, cleric Girolamo Savonarola, Napoleon Bonaparte, Vladimir Lenin, Joseph Stalin (Iosif Vissarionovich Dzhugashvili), Benito Mussolini, Adolf Schickelgruber-Hiedler (Hitler), Mao Zedong, Kim Il Sung, Augusto Pinochet, and in recent years; Mobutu Sese Seko (Joseph Desire Mobutu), Ho Chi Minh, Pol Pot, Saddam Hussein, Muammar Ghaddafi, cleric seyed Ruhollah Moussavi-Mostafavi (Khomeini), his successor, seyed Ali Hosseini (Khamenei), Bashar al Assad and a host of other unknown and so far unlisted enslavers, tyrants and murderers both in the past and the present. All claimed and claim to be the finality of wisdom.

A case to remember is that of one of the infamous madman in Germany between the years 1933 and 1945 who planned a systematic murder of a nation who in his delusional state of mind, were unfit to live since they were either non-gentiles or of not being contributive to life and living. May one ask this individual, with virtually little educational eruditions, as to who endowed him with the gift to judge as to who was and who was not worthy of living.

The enslaver Nazi leader had ordained the cold-blooded murder of Jewish men, women and children as his mission in life. He was the example of an enslaver. This was a deliberate murder of millions who were gassed to death for practicing their religious beliefs. Shocking scenes are many, but most brutal of all was Jewish mothers bravely carrying their infants in their arms to meet certain deaths.

A little more than sixty-five years later, after this mass murderer and enslaver in history committed suicide on April 30, 1945, an article dated August 24, 2010 by journalist Jean-Paul Mulders and historian Marc Vermeeren in the Daily Mail said the dictator's DNA tests proved that he too, just as the millions of his victims was a Jew. His DNA (through thirty-nine surviving family members and an Austrian farmer; his cousin identified as Norbert H.) is most commonly found in the Berbers of Morocco, Tunisia, Algeria and Libya as well as in 18 to 20 percent of Ashkenazi and 8.6 to 30 percent of Sephardic people. On the same day

"The Telegraph" wrote that the non-German dictator who was born in Austria "had Jewish and African roots," DNA tests show. Several other newspapers including the Bloomberg News, Haaretz, Jerusalem Post, Daily Sun, Huffington and the Post all printed the same article.

"One can from this postulate that the dictator was related to people whom he despised," Mr. Mulders, additionally wrote in the Belgian magazine "Knack."

This master of deceit and crime could be called one of the major mind-molesters of history where he mentally enslaved millions and millions of people to perform crimes against humanity on his behalf. He had successfully enslaved approximately seventy five million people by 1940, a people whose nationality he did not even share and whose language he haltingly spoke, save for a few repeated mantras of hate that he was groomed in and memorized. A great portion of the German population who despised him made the supreme sacrifice and courageously stood up against him.

What is striking is that the mass murderer did not know any of the millions of innocent men, women and children he had ordered murdered.

Strangely enough, the final destiny of nearly all these cruel individuals is painful. Except for two known tyrants (cleric Seyed Ali Hosseini Khamenei and Bashar al-Assad) who are still alive, the rest had painful endings; suicide, execution, prolonged illness, abandonment, sufferings and imprisonment in the least.

The most important description of a toppled despotic ruler when arrested and brought to justice is very similar to others already undergoing trial. All present a similar scene, the ability to transfer their beings from a monster to a docile, god loving, pious and a harmless individual while in the process of being tried for a variety of crimes, from mass murder to treason and sedition. Feigning absolute innocence, they have no response to any of the charges. They only blame the mass media, certain democratic governments and reactionary forces.

In modern times, the sane world has witnessed the changed countenance and demeanors of the ex-Yugoslavian strongman, those in Africa and in Far East Asia at the time of their trial.

Pol Pot, the most murderous man in the past five decades could be seen with his hands folded, perhaps until his last breath, while Slobodan Milosevic, Radovan Karadzic, Momcillo Krajisnik, Ratko Mladic and a host of other ex-Yugoslavian individuals, Liberian Charles Taylor and many more appear depressed but never regretting their acts.

The tyrants first enslaved a willing group who were to become their henchmen to launch a murderous attack on those who rejected their rule. The tyrant thus created unabated bloodshed on his opponents and those whom he personally despised through his enslaved followers.

One may have also heard or read about the consequences of the rule of these two types of tyrants; the religious and the non religious types, whether in uniform or in civilian attire. The results in all the cases are virtually the same: death, destruction, bloodshed and mayhem.

Individuals from Nero to Ratko Mladic were the cause of slavery of nearly a billion lives resulting in the death of a hundred million lives or even much more! Enslaved faithful and believers of these masters of crime performed the gory task of killing other people.

The clergyman despot repeatedly invokes heavenly interventions and blessings for those who die for his causes and beliefs and incarcerates hundreds of thousands of intellectuals. He orders assassinations in the country he supposedly administers and directs death to those away from the country who may have been fortunate enough to escape his onslaught. He throws his enemies, real or imagined into the most appalling conditions in primitive dungeons and subjects them to horrendous brutalities, including state-sponsored rapes, and tortures. He will suggest such acts as being fully permissible in the teachings of his belief and religion, which he imposes on the public through his armed thugs or at gunpoint.

The tyrannical cleric in Tehran, orders what the people should eat, how they should eat, what to wear, what to say and how to appear; even their hairstyle! His ordinances are very simple, just what the subjugated people are required to do and not to do. Paid thugs brutally implement his orders. He seldom smiles, except on very rare occasions to confuse the general population into thinking that all is well. He always speaks in monologue. He does not ever entertain any form of interviews with the press or journalists. He is above all these; he is not in the least amenable to anyone for any of his deeds, however cruel and contrary to any acceptable society.

On the other hand, the civilian or military counterpart instills fear and chauvinistic emotions within his shackled nation. He demeans the imagined foes, who are actually fellow citizens, as mere pests who deserve to be eliminated. His practices bear similarity with the clergyman. Among those, he seldom smiles or gives an interview. The mass media in the country is glued to his call. They are omnipresent to praise him. This is mental and physical slavery at its peak.

These enslavers have one deed in common, to enslave the population and to force them to labor and produce that which is vital for the continuation of his enslavement of the masses: enough food and services for his personal servitors!

In this midst, let us not forget forced prostitution, which is the other form of slavery. The chains and fetters are not seen, but they are everywhere on the body of the female. Her only duty before dying is to satisfy and to bring income to her owner.

Conclusion has it that this evil trade has various faces, and has been either government sanctioned or individually practiced. There arrives a juncture where the global community and major governments of the world, who claim to be monitoring and combating slavery, are well aware of this evil trade. Nonetheless, they pretend otherwise, or lessen its importance or go to the extent of using such a phrase as "stray incidents" here and there.

The Global Slavery Index on October 17, 2013 reported that the global slavery figure stood at thirty million. This only meant those in chains and human bondage. The Report did not disclose those trafficked and forced into prostitution or held in forced labor. In India alone, there are more than twenty five million "damned" beings, according to Social Workers and the various groups fighting child labor, forced prostitution and beggary. In China, the figure is not less, with the nearly five million prison inmates throughout the country who also live in perpetual slavery until their date of release.

Just westward in Pakistan there are nearly five million child laborers (slaves) in addition to at least a similar number in forced labor and slavery and a bit north-west to it in Afghanistan, children are enslaved as property. Eastward in Bangladesh, it has been suggested that nearly five million child laborers are brutalized in rendering slave labor with just a few morsels of food. In Thailand, the case of young girls abducted and forced into prostitution is well know and in Nepal, the young girls are sold in the market to traffickers who smuggle them to India and elsewhere to serve the pleasures of rich Indians.

The world stands in silence while in virtually all the countries in Africa, this sorrowful trade needs no elaboration.

A more detailed study of the nations will be dealt in proceeding pages, and a glimpse of what mankind is capable of doing against mankind albeit the efforts of the so-called International Organizations dealing with Human Rights.

Undoubtedly, this incurable ailment has been going on for millenniums; perhaps every square kilometer of the earth's surface; everywhere, in every country, in every city and town and village and communities and continues to this very hour!

Since the past two decades, the global communities and people have suddenly awakened from their indifference to more vigorously husband the cause of the fallen and the forgotten! In the past several years, even several governments guilty of either enslaving or being irrelevant to enslavement have shown interest to fight the ever increasing slavery worldwide. Cambodia, Myanmar, Vietnam to name a few in Far East Asia and India. In Iran, the people are fighting back against theocracy and the clergymen with little or no effect. They are mercilessly crushed, while the global communities watch by passively. Costa Rica, Venezuela, Panama and Brazil in Central and South America have doubled their efforts to rescue thousands from slavery. Their achievements so far, although immense and worthy of praise, is still negligible.

Speaking of governments who claim to fight slavery while at the same time being identified as the ones grossly guilty for state-sponsored enslavement, one can observe an abyssal degree of sheer hypocrisy. Most of the countries championing the cause of human freedom, at some International Organization have a genuine approach.

Of notable interest are some of those governments with a power of "Veto" at the United Nations who may be identified as the ones reaping a harvest from "forced labor;" a more "beatified" form of the word "slavery." The banality and voracity of mankind as being the main causes to continue this "trade in evil" for financial gains can never be underestimated!

One feels startled to note that in this age; in this very moment, out of 243 countries in the world 181 countries have been documented to be affected by human trafficking in one way or the other. People are trafficked from 127 countries to be enslaved in 137 countries in one form or the other. This has effectively affected every continent and every form of economic activity from farming to industries and prostitution, enslavement and bondage as long as they are alive!

A detailed insight into this shameful act will question the validity of claims of several governments sworn to combat slavery. A shocking report by a Human-Watch Society in the Netherlands, which requests anonymity, claims that in their research for the last thirty months, in Asia, Europe and the American Continent, an unbelievable 88 percent of those human beings trafficked die before they reach 30! On an average, four hundred young girls with falsified birthdates arrive daily in ten major cities in the European Continent. Geneva, Zurich, Paris, Brussels, Rome, Milan, London, Copenhagen, Amsterdam and Vienna are determined to be the main ports of entry of this "human cargo" to serve the rich.

In Western Europe, those that are enslaved in a more benign manner for prostitution, live to be in their 50's to ultimately die of painful venereal diseases. The victims of mankind's lust have no means to undergo medical attention.

The women are simply discarded on reaching their thirtieth birthday and forced out. New groups of young girls, some underage but with doctored documents, arrive at regular intervals from every country thinkable. Some are spirited to Israel on their immediate arrival in any European city, their only destination in South West Asia. Most of the human cargo, reminiscent of transportation of unfortunate human beings in trains to their definite demise in death camps during the Second World War; now arrive in airplanes. Most are transported to the Netherlands, Ireland, Belgium, Switzerland, France, Italy and Germany. Canada is also a point of destination but in lesser numbers.

The least number are taken to the USA (from other than the American Continent) thanks to difficulties and restrictions in obtaining Visas but not for those in other parts of the Continent itself, since they are smuggled through the Mexican border. That number is staggering.

After serving the lust of the rich and the privileged for a few years at the most, the lesser privileged prepare to die as if through some divine intuition. Their remains are quietly disposed off, as if they never existed. They (the exploiters) have their own crematoriums—rarely are the unfortunates buried. They are not even considered a statistic. "Their death is not an event, it is considered as a 'natural process' to make way for younger ones, a generation who is already waiting," an expert with the Society for the Protection of Enslaved Women in Amsterdam stated.

Investigations and research has shown that the female victims are kidnapped, sold, traded and bartered in various forms. Their price in India and Thailand and the Philippines are far below the price of edible flesh: chicken, pork, beef and mutton in most countries of Europe, not to mention dog meat in the Philippines, China, Vietnam, Cambodia, Laos and the Koreas! Even payments made to buy a pet, whether a cat, a dog or a bird costs more.

Imagine the incredible value of a human being weighing some sixty kilograms (some 132 pounds) sold at retail price for a mere One hundred thirty two US dollars! This computes to one dollar per pound of a human flesh.

In South Sudan, men, women and children from the Dinka Tribe, regardless of their weight, are sold each for fifteen US dollars to Arabs from the North and other North African countries! This business has no known definition, job description or any form of standard practice procedure. There is no booklet, manual or guide for crime. Those involved in this heinous act perform their duties as if it flows naturally within their scope of thoughts and talents. Unfortunately, the United Nations and its affiliates are still supposedly researching and investigating this saga.

Every announcement made by the United Nations dealing with the question of slavery states that the Secretary General and those in the Council on Human Rights and several committees dealing with slavery appear to be comfortably pleased at the pace of work and the steps taken so far. More funds are eagerly allocated for these self-styled experts who consider their contributions as simply outstanding and worthy of praise.

The larger majority of these "experts" and higher echelons of the United Nations are rarely found to be behind their desks. They are busily travelling, or are on an extended vacation or are away responding to invitations from dignitaries from various parts of the world. Those same dignitaries that are identified as defaulters on Human Rights play host to these experts.

It is a known fact that the majority of the employees at the United Nations are employed through acquaintances or friends. It is an accepted fact that the employment system of the United Nations is the most corrupt in the world! One does not fail to find drunken employees in the corridors of this Organization in Geneva, often responding to your question with a slurred speech. They also appear to speak haltingly in any of the major languages required: English, French, Spanish, Chinese, or even Portuguese. One may note that after the demise of Dag Hammarskjold, there was not a single Secretary General of the United Nations who spoke either English or French in an audible manner.

One could barely comprehend what U Thant or Kurt Waldheim or individuals like Javier Peres de Cuellar, Boutros-Ghali or Kofi Annan murmured. One has to strain his mental faculties to understand what the present Secretary General Ban ki-moon wants to say. This odious development will always remain there!

Some existing and irrefutable developments afflicting regions deeply involved in slave trade have never come up for discussion at any United Nations Human Rights Sub-committees. On many occasion, India, Pakistan, Nepal, Bangladesh as the source countries and Arab Sheikhdoms in the Persian Gulf as destination countries are not even mentioned. They are just omitted without any explanation.

Shocking news such as the report of young Nepali girls, some as young as nine years old smuggled into neighboring India and sold for a mere two thousand Indian Rupees; equal to some thirty five United States dollars has never been discussed seriously, just a passing remark has been made of this grizzly trade. No attempts are made to discuss the topic that once these Nepali girls are in India; they are re-sold by the trafficker for a hundred percent profit to live in bondage with the new buyer.

The United Nations does not want to touch the subject of this brutal trade, that in India, Nepali girls are re-sold for a mere hundred dollars; bought and sold, traded and bartered like livestock. Their lives are worth that much in the eyes of individuals masquerading as guardians of human beings at the United Nations. One must not expect any form of sanity from the thugs involved in this deed. It has been documented and proved that the average lifespan of such an unfortunate female human being in India is less than thirty. Once they are unwanted they are in the streets, left open to be abused, beaten and even murdered by elements seeking the thrill of killing another human being, for no reason. Their bodies, according to reports witnessed, are simply dumped into a truck, especially designed for this purpose and simply hauled away by the municipality. The destination is usually a furnace and the development is simply termed as "uneventful."

These prematurely dead or even murdered men and women throughout the world have suffered too much to describe, too much to narrate and much more than a human body could bear and tolerate. They were and are transported from one country to another, from one continent to another like postal packages, with promises to have a better life, a prosperous and a healthy life, but instead end dying or murdered in the streets after their physical values to serve are diminished.

Apart from the young Nepalese girls brought into India and forced into a life of slavery and prostitution, each year, hundreds of thousands of underage girls, some as young as six and seven from various parts of India are forced into prostitution. The darker blot is that the indebted parents out of miseries and hardships sell them to professional traders for this purpose. The parents are well aware of the destiny of their children. They do not see their children again.

India claims to be championing the cause of the lesser privileged and the oppressed, but this is the undeniable factuality of human bondage in that country and yet the succeeding governments have enough budgetary considerations for armaments and nuclear weapons.

A moment of absolute silence within us tells us that this eternal stain of shame and disgust upon mankind is not brought unto us by impersonal forces; or through some conspiracy or a diabolical plot from some other Milky Way, another Constellation, another Planet, but by ourselves against ourselves in this very place called Earth. Initially we may conclude and even close the book on this subject, that the battle is lost and mankind is doomed to this "Cosmic Curse." However, a second thought ignites hope—hope that will at least ablate this misery, if not all of a sudden, in stages, but with success.

For the present, the horror continues, it appears that slavery is eternal!

Chapter II

Horror in Detail
(Continent by Continent)

"Be faithful, be vigilant, be untiring in your efforts to break every yoke, and let the oppressed go free. Come what may—cost what it may—inscribe on the banner, which you unfurl to the breeze, as your religious and political motto—"NO COMPROMISE WITH SLAVERY! NO UNION WITH SLAVEHOLDERS."

William Lloyd Garrison

"I swore never to be silent whenever and wherever human beings endure sufferings and humiliation. We must always take sides. Neutrality helps the oppressor, never the victim. Silence encourages the tormentor, never the tormented."

Elie Weasel,
Nobel Peace Prize Laureate and Holocaust survivor

The disease of dominance of a human being on another human being existed and exists everywhere; it is a global misery; a stubborn malady which refuses to heal. Whether five, six or seven continents; the crux of the matter is Slavery; this stubborn scourge on society since time immemorial. As such, the focal points are Africa, Asia, Europe, and North, South and Central America.

Sociologists, psychologists and experts in this field have retreated one by one after a period of arduous research to find ways and means to either ablate or put a total stop to this trade in human bondage and flesh. They have apparently given up! The various Committees related to the

United Nations, Non-Governmental Organizations and Societies spread throughout the world have for decades vowed to bring about the demise of this trade with little or no effect or results. Instead, they have played the role of admonishing the defaulters with a fatherly approach. Promises and hopes virtually vanish, once the delegates submit their reports, which are mostly gratuitous.

Only their feeble and half-hearted reports remain as a testimony of their so-called efforts to place them as championing the cause of the oppressed, the enslaved and those in chains. Beyond this, it is a matter of "Much ado about nothing!" Their respective Government after much fanfare calmly files the reports with a highly publicized promise of a profound investigation into the matter and accordingly appoints another Committee to investigate the reports of the delegate. After that, all the reports become flimsy pieces of paper without any value whatsoever.

Investigating or rather, undertaking a detailed study of this staggering and mind devastating subject beggars a question as to what has been done in the past decades and even beyond that, to bring about some amelioration to mankind's sufferings at the hands of mankind. An immediate result tells that awareness and modernization has had no effect of any form on this act of treachery on human beings by human beings.

The geometrical increase in the world's population has in fact disproportionately increased the number of those in shackles. The increase in percentage of those enslaved is usually played down but appears alarming to the common mind. Private investigations by non governmental organizations in Brazil and several other countries in South America show that the ratio of the number of slaves, vis-à-vis their country's population has shrunk since 2000-2010; while others in Mexico claim it has increased and continues at a horrifying rate, chiefly due to the influx of illegal migrants from several nearby small countries south of Mexico. Brazil has shown a conspicuous degree of prosperity resulting in a better living condition than that which existed before the country's entry into the twenty first century.

Economic and financial exigencies and limitations may be accused of being the villain in this "theater of tragedy" but on examination, this is not so. Mankind's betrayal against mankind has not to come to a sudden stop so easily albeit a better economy.

In order to remedy the ailment it is but inevitable to examine the root causes and the areas affected together with accurate statistics. In most of the source countries for kidnapping and trafficking, the victims destined for slavery elsewhere are rarely documented or registered. If they were ever documented, the subject of slavery could have been more easily dealt with. Far from having any accurate figure and statistics, one has to greatly depend on an unexaggerated and syllogistic hypothesis in arriving at any figure.

The whole subject of disseminating the truth from falsehood and unearthing the existing facts is not only a cumbersome procedure but also that the results may be greatly questionable. As such, largely the subject of exposing the evils of slavery with very correct statistics appears to be a challenge. It is, extensively wrapped in mystery.

Millions or perhaps tens of millions of cases of slavery exist according to official statistics released by the United Nations and at this very moment, it continues to unabatedly increase.

The global figure of thirty million human beings in slavery released in early 2012 appears to be far less than is suspected to be. Experts from India, Pakistan, Bangladesh, Belgium, Switzerland, France, Brazil, Mexico, Israel and Canada put it at an unbelievable figure exceeding one hundred million. They vociferously contest that there are at least five million in Mexico, two million in Brazil, ten million in Pakistan, two million or even more in Russia, ten million in Bangladesh and an overwhelming figure of twenty five million in India. China has an equal number if not more and there are more than ten million in the African Continent. As stated earlier, there are no accurate figures reflecting the total number of human beings in slavery in the world at any given time.

Add to that another tens of million of human beings in bondage, scattered throughout the world. "Were we to examine the number of human beings in all forms of slavery including exploitation and forced labor, this would add to a staggering one hundred and fifty million and more," according to a Human Rights watch group based in Geneva, Switzerland! Such a massive figure of human beings dead but alive, alive but dead! However, this figure may be considered as grossly bloated, and to instead give a figure of one hundred million, although not less, is still staggering to the common mind.

Continent by Continent, country by country, statistics prove the ultimate in horror; the abyssal chasm between those living a normal life and the ones physically existing, but one could eventually blame humankind itself for this incurable disease that spells the total collapse of culture, civilization and human dignity.

It would be unfair to commence the saga of this sickening trade, slavery in a variety of forms, of any country either through alphabetical order or through their infamy and notoriety. It will be examined at least continent by continent to facilitate comprehension of regional developments. Almost all of them would be and could be termed as gross offenders or actively involved in dealing with human beings as commodities to serve the needs of other human beings whether enslavement for labor or for serving human lust.

If hundreds of thousands or millions promoted this vile trade in the past and in the present, then one must also note honorable names that selflessly and valiantly fought and continue to fight this man made evil. While the former comprised of ignorant or semi-literate, vicious, corrupt, heartless, religious bigots and scheming individuals, the latter was and is made of the educated, spiritual and the sane.

Immortal names such as Lord Mansfield, Ignatius Sancho, William Wilberforce, Olaudah Equiano, Jacques Pierre Brissot, Hugh Elliot, Thomas Payne, John Jay, William Lloyd Garrison, Frederick Douglass, Frances Wright, Samuel Sewall, Elijah Parish Lovejoy, Lysander Spooner, John Brown, to name a few, unassumingly and bravely led the unceasing battle against the cowardice of slavery. Of importance is that the subjects of Slavery, Human Bondage including assaults on women's dignity and Human Rights are interdependent and closely related.

In this midst mankind must always remember the historical deed of one person conspicuously important in creating an Institution to defend the Rights of the forgotten, the exploited and those destined to die as mere objects unworthy of anything except to labor for those who have dominance over them, either through wealth, political skullduggery or various forms of authoritarian rule. He was none other that Peter Benenson.

It must be repeated that the subjects of Slavery and Human Bondage are closely knit and are virtually inseparable. Where there is forced prostitution, which is at least 95 percent of all the cases, regardless where the subject, or rather, the victim is underage or of age to decide, the aspect of exploitation of that individual matters and that is enslavement. Which woman, which girl, which member of the feminine gender desires to be enslaved and to have her human dignity assaulted? There is, undoubtedly the factor of enslavement by the unscrupulous ones.

Peter Benenson (Solomon . . . 1921-2005) founder of Amnesty International (1961) in early 2001 said: "For the last fifty years, I have taken keenness to the subject of slavery and took a very active role, often in private, to fight its cruelty," in a discussion with his friend, tutor and mentor Mr. Auden (Wystan Hugh Auden 1907-1973) in 1950. (In a meeting by the Author with Mr. Alexandre Hay, President of the International Red Cross in early July 1984 in Geneva). Both also discussed the worsening situation of Human Rights in China (then under Mao) and the unbridled trade in human beings in India and East and West Pakistan. (East Pakistan was to seek independence as Bangladesh on March 26, 1971).

Wystan Hugh Auden, the noted Anglo-American poet in early 1970 told a group of visitors at his residence that the strangulation of the public in the Balkans and satellite Soviet Bloc countries was appalling and beyond human imagination.

Mass imprisonments for using prisoners for projects under humane conditions is one subject and utilizing the labors of prisoners as slaves is a different topic. In China, harsh treatment awaits all prisoners!

On the topic of Slavery and Human Rights affecting the Subcontinent, in early 2002, Peter Benenson reflected reservation as to the degree of success in muzzling slavery and indenture for Pakistan and Bangladesh. He stated that excepting India, where a measure of democracy exists, there is little hope for Pakistan and Bangladesh, Afghanistan, Iran, Syria and Turkey. The so-called heads of state and the ruling hierarchies are the self-appointed Prison Wardens with absolute right on the lives of the prisoners. What is most appalling is in Iran, where the Muslim clergy, claim and insist that Islamic Teachings permit severe punishments of prisoners and extracting slave labor. In almost all these places, deaths of individuals while working under extreme conditions are not even registered.

> "Poverty is not an accident. Like Slavery and apartheid, it is man-made and can be removed by the actions of human beings."
>
> Nelson Mandela.

Wherever poverty abounds and people are held backward for ulterior motives and agendas, that place appears to be a thriving ground for enslavement and human bondage. Whether in state-run prisons, labor camps, brothels, farms and industrial units, the unscrupulous ones are ubiquitously there to transform the omnipresent suffering masses into slaves. Such locations on earth are not necessarily overpopulated regions but those reeling in poverty where the common human being's very life and existence, whether a male or a female is more susceptible to be bought and sold for a token amount. That freshly inducted individual in the world of slavery is promised a dry crust of bread at minimum to survive and a space for the night. His or her life enters a new phase on earth; to labor, sweat, be beaten, tortured, mistreated and to live a brief tormented life.

An unexaggerated insight of this horror devastates the very mind, body and soul of any individual with moral values and spiritual approach to life. The conscience of the dominator, those born to rule, dominate, enslave and destroy, can never be understood, even by the best psychiatrist and psychologist.

AFRICA

The African continent occupies 20.4 percent of the total land area and includes fifty-five countries with a total population of 1.1 billion inhabitants.

Almost all the countries in this continent are involved in various forms of slavery. Bride buying, debt bondage, human trafficking, sexual slavery, child labor and outright slavery of human beings are the known forms.

Although slavery is prohibited in all of the African countries, it is a well known fact that some form of slavery is practiced in Mali, Islamic Republic of Mauritania, Uganda, Rwanda, Senegal, South Africa, Zimbabwe, Sudan, Ethiopia, Niger, Cameroon, Eritrea, Gambia, Gabon, Benin, Togo, Burkina Faso, Ghana and in the Democratic Republic of Congo. The United Nations' various Committees on Human Rights have singled out these countries as paying little or no attention to the gravity of human sufferings inflicted on indentured slaves. Investigative reports have revealed that in these countries there may be at least ten million people in fetters or in various forms of slavery. Far-fetched figures have put the figure of slavery in various forms in the African continent to exceed 25 million. Hundreds of thousands of girls as young as ten are kidnapped from villages or bought from their parents and trafficked to other parts of the continent while nearly fifty thousand are smuggled into various European countries each year.

The Society of Jurors based in Geneva claimed that inter-state trafficking in Africa exceeds two hundred thousand a year.

In the north of the continent, Morocco, Tunisia, Algeria, Libya and Egypt are also involved in this notorious trade. The majority of young girls, aged between nine and fifteen are kidnapped or purchased from their parents to smuggle them to the Sheikhdoms in the Persian Gulf. Combined research papers, including documents from the Sub-Committee of Human Rights at the United Nations in Geneva bears witness that a minimum of one hundred thousand girls with falsified papers are escorted to wealthy Arabs in Saudi Arabia, the U.A.E., Kuwait and Bahrain each year.

All said, due to the absence of any official identification papers including passports, verification of the movement and trafficking of the victims from the various African States to other countries is nearly impossible. Most of the statistics come through either independent journalists or local welfare groups in those particular countries.

ASIA

India

> "Man is born free and everywhere he is in chains."
>
> Jean Jacques Rousseau

India is described as being the second-most populous country with a population exceeding 1.2 billion and being the most populous democracy in the world. Virtually all political parties in India underline the urgency of fighting any form of slavery in the country during the election years, proving they are aware of the issue, but rarely follow this case once elected. Human trafficking in India dates back even before the independence of India from Britain in August 15, 1947. The British rarely tried the defaulters considering it an internal affair of the Indian families.

However, in recent years, the public have taken unto themselves the task of fighting the menace of slavery in its various forms. Success, although slow, has come to several regions of the vast country.

Several global organizations combating slavery including the United States State Department Trafficking in Persons Report, dated June 2009 reported that India is a source, destination, and transit country for men, women and children trafficked for the purposes of slave labor and commercial sexual exploitation. Internal forced labor may constitute India's largest trafficking problem; men, women and children in debt bondage are forced to work in industries such as brick kilns, rice mills, agriculture, and embroidery factories. Children are also subjected to forced labor as factory workers, domestic servants, beggars and agricultural workers.

The figures reflected for the victims of various forms of slavery in India are controversial and extensively questionable. However, it has to be borne in mind that the country's population is more than 1.2 billion! Since no dependable form of statistics are available, efforts have been made to present those figures that are logically acceptable. Various groups and organizations have presented numbers differing from the others.

The U.S. State Department Trafficking in Persons Report in their annual report on global slavery in 2009 could not come up with a definite or even an approximate figure as to the number of human beings that could be considered as slaves in India. "Millions, just millions," was the response by an official from the United States State Department related to Human Trafficking, who declined to identify himself.

Prostitution; the other face of slavery, is improperly documented and often underestimated, not only in India but also throughout the world when it comes to the topic of slavery.

The Ministry of Women and Child Development of India reported in early 2007 that nearly 2.8 million prostitutes existed in India of which dealers and brokers forced nearly 50 percent into this trade.

Reports are conflicting and so are the figures, but what is true are the alarming and shocking statistics. In the same year, nearly a dozen private Societies and Groups secretly sprung up in India, some managed by Missionaries and Charities ostensibly formed to save and rescue underage children, from slavery, prostitution and forced labor, some as young as eight years old.

In early 2003 Mrs. Vipula Kadri the founder of Save the Children India, stated that more than two million underage children, below the age of twelve, are enslaved into a life of prostitution. She claimed that more than 40 percent of nearly five million prostitutes scattered throughout the country were below eighteen years of age. Mrs. Vipula Kadri, recipient of several awards by the Indian government, also mentioned that often father, mother and the children worked side by side for a few morsel of bread, not exceeding twenty-five cents in US currency per day. Violence was also used against them in front of each other. A few disgruntled and problematic slaves were in leashes most of the day while they toiled, except for a few hours at night. Investigation of those who escaped the misery stated that the enslaved people would obligingly allow fetters and chains to be put on them. "This is the ultimate of shame," she said.

The figures for forced labor and various forms of slavery provided by the eleven various charitable societies formed by volunteers throughout India were virtually the same, given a 2 or 3 percent difference. One differed in the figure, which added another two million as involved in prostitution in private homes, undetected by law. Most of these Societies, which are in Mumbai, Kolkata, Chennai, New Delhi, Hyderabad and Bhopal, requested anonymity for security reasons. In the addendum of the same report, a harrowing figure of fifteen to sixteen million enslaved people, some as young as eight, working in quarries, brick kilns, cattle and pig farms in the most shocking conditions was mentioned.

The two-page report of the Ministry of Women and Child development only presented statistics! It made no mention, directly or indirectly, of what measures were being taken to combat this national calamity.

"Nearly six years later in mid 2013, the Ministry falsely claimed the same figure as the one in 2007," said an employee of the Ministry who requested anonymity. Without any documents to support their claim, the reports stated that the situation was under control and people themselves had found professions that are more productive. This being said, the question arises as to how could people who were forced into such a life be able to search for a better profession when their very lives and existence were in fetters and chains?

More Societies sprung up by the end of 2011 to combat slavery in India. They became financially assisted, although very insufficiently. "Most of the financial help comes from well known movie stars, some octogenarians and those whose names I am not at liberty to mention. Some are the common public desirous to perform a benign deed," said Paresh Rawal, a film actor who has been actively involved throughout the country in identifying slaves to be rescued.

The majority of volunteers sworn to combat slavery in India do not belong to any official group or society. They belong to different professions; some are Sociologists, University Lecturers and Attorneys. Popular movie stars have joined hands to smash the chains of slavery and bondage in India. Among them, the late Feroz Khan, Akshay Kumar, Paresh Rawal, Anil Kapoor and Vishwanath "Nana" Patekar who have vowed to fight this evil until their last breath. All have sworn to continue their war irrespective of threats to their lives. Even retired Army and Naval Officers of the Indian

Armed forces courageously volunteered to save their fellow brethren by visiting far-flung regions of the country to counsel and help families in financial distress who may be tempted to sell their children to scheming traffickers.

In the summer of 2013, the several anti-slavery societies in India countered the claims and figures of the Ministry of Women and Child Development for the year 2012 as deceitful. Government reports stated that the number of child prostitution throughout the country as mentioned in the report of the Ministry of Women and Child Development was only 15 percent underage girls out of 2.8 million in 2007 with the rest being adults. The Ministry stressed that between the years 2007 and 2013, the figures were virtually unchanged! Anti Slavery Societies throughout the country challenged the figures claiming nearly five million, with at least 40 percent of them being underage girls. Nearly a hundred thousand of them were trafficked from Nepal while another similar figure was from Bangladesh.

The number of slaves of all types throughout India, which excludes prostitution for those within the required age group, now, exceeds twenty million. This figure includes forced prostitution including adults and underage, forced labor, slave ownership and various other forms of human dominations in India.

Labor Reports of the government are sheer phantasm! The Ministry of Women and Child Development is a government undertaking. What else one should expect from them, except to embellish the miseries of the public and present a pleasant report to please the world. The situation is horrible; just too horrible of any form of mention. To control this terrible calamity, it will take at least two decades or more.

"We have a prostitute population of nearly five million; this equals 80 percent of the entire population of Switzerland! Now is the time for an emergency decree by the government to take immediate steps," said Dr. P. Kalekar, a former biologist.

"We spend billions every year for armaments, updating and further developing missiles and nuclear weapons and this is the sorrowful condition of the general population," said Prof. Virgil Matthews, a former lecturer in Philosophy.

Several Independent Societies in India are making all efforts to prevent the government agents from falsifying the statistics and presenting favorable reports to the public and the world. Reports state that those opposing Government statistics on slavery in India are branded as traitors, liars and in the pay of foreign powers.

"But of course, those involved in this cowardly act are rich and their wealth pays off the law; the same law that has sworn to protect us," said Feroz Khan one of the most prominent and respected movie stars of India. Mr. Khan, in failing health, in early 2007 made a dramatic plea to all his Indian compatriots to combine all their resources to fight slavery.

These twenty or so Anti Slavery Societies presently operate in major States of India where prostitution, forced and slave labor actively and unabatedly thrive. It has been determined that nearly 85 percent of the present ills in the entire country are concentrated in twelve States; Uttar Pradesh, Bihar, Maharashtra, West Bengal, Andhra Pradesh, Tamil Nadu, Orissa, Kerala, Karnataka, Gujarat, Madhya Pradesh, and Rajasthan. The combined population of these twelve States exceeds a billion human beings! The entire population of the country exceeds 1.210 billion (2011 census) and keeps rising uncontrollably.

"It is impossible to closely monitor the situation or visit everywhere whenever there is an information of violation of Human Rights; especially Slavery. It is widespread. We would need at least two thousand volunteers for every State and with a sufficient budget," said Anil Kapoor, well-known Indian movie actor, who spearheads a group to hunt down slave traders and traffickers.

The twelve States earlier mentioned are also among the densely populated ones in the country. Research has shown that the enslavers have transported most of their victims from any one of these States to another, preferable to the adjoining ones in the belief that they would be isolated and away from relatives or friends who may want to rescue them or even approach the law.

"It is recently that law enforcement authorities have decided to diligently support our cause. We are not official in the sense that we are just Humane Societies. We are 'brotherly and sisterly vigilantes' striving to rescue and free our brethren from chains," We do not carry any weapon or 'nightsticks' or even handcuffs," said Feroz Khan on August 15, 2006 coinciding with India's Independence Day.

Feroz Khan also said that certain factors create a challenge to categorize those under slavery. A good percentage of those who could be categorized as slaves do not mind to continue their lives as long as they receive a bowl of rice and some bread to labor for hours in farms and cattle breeding centers, especially in pig farms under the most deplorable conditions.

Large numbers of people have been smuggled out of Indian borders and taken overland to Malaysia and elsewhere for the opulent and the rich. Most of them have not seen the outside of the houses they work in. The majority are said to be young girls, some as young as twelve! They are prudently kept within the confines of the property as long as they are able to work. It has been suggested that they are discreetly buried on the grounds of the properties where they die.

Sreyashi Dastidar writing in "The Telegraph," October 16, 2007, under the heading "Never too young to be sold" wrote on the circumstances dealing with kidnapping and trading in slavery wishes the circumstances were the same, but they seldom are.

He argued as to how does one equate a girl lured away from a village in Meghalaya to a brothel in Delhi with the one pushed into bidi-binding (small hand-rolled cigarettes infused with various flavors) by her own parents just so there is enough money to feed all the mouths in the family?

Apart from the courageous writings of Dastidar, Dan McDougall wrote an article in "The Observer" on October 27, 2007 where he lambasted the fashion giant "Gap" for its direct and indirect encouragement of children's slavery in India, some as young as ten!

"Child workers, some as young as ten, have been found to be working in textile factory in conditions close to slavery to produce clothes that appear destined for Gap Kids, a successful clothes manufacturer for children," McDougall wrote.

Rogues in search of fame and name have endorsed and even praised the quality of the garments produced in India for Gap. So-called celebrities like Madonna (Madonna Louise Ciccone), Lenny Kravitz, Sarah Jessica Parker, among others have made statements suggesting the benefits of buying this line of products sold by Gap. McDougall also reported that in 2004, Gap, admitted in private as to who produced these items, their average ages and the amount they were paid. At least half of them were children under the age of fifteen.

One of the most appalling situations in India is the topic of Child "carpet slaves!" In 2001 it was estimated that between a quarter million and a third of a million of children, as young as five years old are openly kidnapped from their villages and are held in captivity and forced to labor on looms for a few dried crusts of bread with onion and salt. By early 2014, the number had increased by 20 percent. Their forced work period was between ten and twelve hours a day. Devoid of any medical attention, a report stated that most were put to death, rather than be given any form of medical care since the business of the enslavers would be exposed. Whether Hindus or Muslims, these children were cremated. Nevertheless, even after being exposed, the Central Government in Delhi is too busy caring for its image abroad by participating in every Sub-committee meeting on Human Rights and Anti-Slavery Conferences.

"These are the known and discovered situations. I say without any hesitation that there are about two million underage children, simply snatched from their parents to be taken and 'inducted' into a life of misery and slavery," said the spouse of a very prominent movie star of India who requested anonymity.

A close study of the Child "carpet slave" in India throws light on the fact that nearly ten million carpets and rugs of various sizes and designs are manufactured in India, each year, using child slavery. Their number has been put at anywhere between a million and a million and half by the end of 2013 and are mostly centered in Uttar Pradesh, Maharashtra, Jammu and Kashmir, and Gujarat. The carpets are sold from four thousand

Indian Rupees (some 80 US dollars) to twenty thousand Indian Rupees (some 400 US dollars), with a good number of them ending in Europe and the USA. The enslaver-entrepreneur invests a mere amount of 5 percent of the total amount of sales of the finished product.

In 2013, major newspapers in India reported that more than 25 percent of India's economy depends upon the slave labor of children, which equals to nearly 75 million youngsters with an average age of thirteen! A confidential report claimed that at least 20 percent of the enslaved victims rarely reach their twentieth birthday. If they are fortunate enough to escape the torments and miseries, they may expect to live another five or six years. Years of untreated health conditions continue to deteriorate but to a lower pace, given the fact that there are sufficient numbers of government managed health clinics and hospitals throughout the country. However, it is too late. Substandard living conditions finally take their toll. The innocent child now grown up is doomed to die prematurely. Slavery has caused his death.

Professor Sheotaj Singh, co-founder of a Delhi based rehabilitation centre and school for rescued child slaves, said that as long as cut-price embroidered goods were sold in stores across Britain, America, Continental Europe and elsewhere in the West, there would be a problem with unscrupulous subcontractors using children.

"It is obvious what the attraction is here for Western conglomerates," he told The Observer. "India offers the global economy the world's cheapest labor, and this is the saddest thing of all the horrors that arise from Delhi's fifteen thousand inadequately regulated garment factories."

Indian film star Anil Kapoor who has been espousing the cause of exploited children for several years said that each year between three hundred and six hundred thousand children are reported missing each year in India. It is a known fact that as many as two million children are trafficked each year and sent to other parts of the country to serve as slaves. Another half a million are brought through the porous borders of Bangladesh and Nepal. A report by the Universal Registration Plan in India said that the global number of missing children annually is anywhere between fifty five million to sixty million. The more unfortunate part of this development is that nearly all are turned into one form of slave or another. Millions disappear each year globally. Many are never found. The Registration Plan believes that once the children are registered it reduces their vulnerability to human rights violations.

Major cities in the States of Maharashtra, Bengal, Madhya Pradesh, Karnataka, Gujarat, Tamil Nadu, Andhra Pradesh and Orissa have become the centers for what has been termed as "enslaved begging," a term unheard of before. Here young boys and girls, the majority of who have been molested, beaten and even punished for under-earning are initially taught the art of begging and stealing; a throwback to the writings of Charles Dickens' "Oliver Twist," and then sent to "work." Here the "Fagins" of the play are ruthless gangsters and hooligans who have most impudently set up centers for the victims, usually kidnapped or bought, from the poverty-stricken parents of the victims or their family members in the absence of parents! Their average age range is between eight to twelve years.

A telephone conversation with an official of The Save the Children India, who requested anonymity, claimed that nearly a million and a half children are forced into this form of slavery. This means that a million children more or less are deprived of any form of health care, nourishment, clothing and above all, education. Documented studies proved that at least 10 percent of them during the first four years die due to illness and various forms of pediatric ailments. New victims are added to the army of young beggars and thieves daily, to replace those who have died or simply vanished from their posts. What is astonishing is that the thugs have an elaborate system to dispose of their bodies without registering the children's death. They have their own crematoriums, some of which are located right behind their so-called dormitories for the night.

"The amount brought to the criminals by these innocent victims add up to anywhere between a quarter to a third of a billion US dollars annually! This is a new horror," a report from the Universal Birth Registration Plan said.

Documents presented showed young boys and girls, some scantily dressed, others shabbily dressed, aggressively begging or stealing from groceries. One who managed to escape told social workers in the city of Kolkata that if any boy or girl brought back less than the amount earmarked by their bosses, they would be either beaten or gang-molested.

In May 2009, Paul Bernish, a popular member of the Founding Board of the Underground Railroad Freedom Center and also the Director of Antislavery and Human Trafficking Initiatives startled the world when he reported that there are as many as 100 million people in India involved in trafficking related activities.

In early 2006, the "Save the Children India" Organization reported that business was booming for male clients who prefer ten to twelve year old girls. "The soaring number of prostitutes in India believed to have contracted HIV in India's brothels has helped give India the second-largest number of people living with HIV/AIDS in the world, just behind South Africa. Yet the trafficking from Nepal, Bangladesh and from the rural areas of India into the brothels of the big city is a blight that has gone unnoticed amongst India's politicians and police forces," the report said.

The largest and probably the world's biggest known brothel operated in a place called Kamatipura in Mumbai (Bombay) with tens of thousands of registered prostitutes. By 2009, the vast red light district, which housed prostitutes since 1795, was dismantled. Prostitution did not end there. At its peak, this region housed some fifty thousand prostitutes. The shanty dwellings were to be high-rise construction projects. The prostitutes were moved to other places. Less than a hundred people owned these brothels. Twice or more this figure now operate in private homes scattered throughout the vast city with a population exceeding twelve million.

The suburban district of Mumbai is one of the largest districts in the country by population. According to the 2011 census, the urban and the suburban population stood at more than ninety three million. Apart from several industrial units producing heavy engineering goods employing millions within the suburban districts of Mumbai, enslaved prostitution and slaves also form the other majority of those employed. Nearly a quarter million prostitutes cater to nearly a hundred million people in this region alone.

Statistics have proved that the other large industry in India appears to be child slavery, forced prostitution, kidnapping, murder and other forms of ills afflicting this country—and India claims to be a technologically advanced nuclear State, regularly developing long-range missiles and modern weapons of mass destruction.

In the cities of Kolkata, Delhi, Chennai, Mumbai, Hyderabad, Ahmadabad, Indore, Bhopal, Kanpur and Lucknow, millions of young girls are enslaved and forced into a life of prostitution. Their lives end at the age of thirty or even less! The young boys on the other hand, appear to be doomed the very moment they are kidnapped and taken to "Training Camps" to be versed in various professions; to work in these sectors: from carpets, rugs, shoes, metal and leather works, lumber, mining, farming, quarries or to the simple but dangerous art of stealing and housebreaking.

The stronger ones are taught the art of murder; from shooting to stabbing, but the latter form is often employed. Guns are rarely provided to individual slaves since ballistic tests may reveal the ownership or the type of weapon. Hence, swords, daggers and sharp edged weapons are provided. The killers will be used for murder-for-hire when deemed strong enough to commit murder. When "deployed" for the task and if arrested for the crime, they are not in a position to give names. They are murdered in prison cells by unknown hands!

Those in private homes are young enslaved girls from various parts of the country. A volunteer for the "Save the Children India" asking anonymity, in early 2014, said; "I am paying more importance, to the present day children who are enslaved into this trade. There are at least five million enslaved prostitutes in India, regardless their age, with fifty or more percent of them being very young."

Justice Department documents, including mass media news prove that the Indian government is well aware of this terrible and incurable challenge affecting the country. Still, it is not too late. Perhaps a few billion dollars could arrest this calamity and a few billion more could be spent to rehabilitate the affected ones. All told, there is no guarantee that this form of enslavement could be brought to a halt in the immediate near future. Criminal elements and thugs come into the picture every day. There are gang leaders who commit this gruesome crime of kidnapping, enslaving and even killing those who refuse to be enslaved.

Research showed that there are groups who have been involved in trafficking and enslaving children, both boys and girls in almost every State of the country. The rampant and unbridled trade in slavery and its various forms including using the slaves to murder will ultimately bring the Indian society to its knees. For the present, no known means can be formulated to cure this man-made curse except for the Indian government to embark on a serious footing to combat this evil within a given time-frame so as to further prevent the total collapse and destruction of the very fabric of Indian society.

China: "The most orderly form of Slavery"

> "We are still savages at heart and wear our thin uniform of civilization awkwardly."
>
> John Bernard Shaw

The world's most populous country perhaps has the most explanation to give to the International Community in terms of its gross misuse of mankind's existence on earth within its territory but it would never be so. China does not feel any need to respond to global criticism for practicing open slavery as a part of its doctrine of Economic Growth and prosperity. It feels that it is a necessary practice to combat the evils of Imperialism, Colonialism and Capitalism.

Dismissing any allegations, the Chinese Commercial Attaché at the United Nations in Geneva in late 2013 claimed that the skills and labor of an individual who has productive potentials is used in production for the benefit of the State, which translates into the benefit of the people and the workers. He said; "Force is sometimes needed to achieve this and this is also beneficial to the individual who is wrongfully classified as forced to render Slave labor."

The United States is the largest purchaser of Chinese products regardless of the conditions they are produced. In 2006, Walmart imported 26.7

billion dollars of goods from China while the amount for the year 2013 stood above 30 billion dollars.

Walmart is the most corrupt enslaver on earth. They operate more than 11,000 stores supposedly employing more than two million unfortunate employees and nearly fifty thousand high-salaried officials paid in hundreds of thousands or millions of dollars a year while the ordinary employees are paid minimum wages obliging them to beg the Government for support. Workers are hired and dismissed every hour. No individual is ever safe working in Walmart. Only the Store Managers and their lackeys feel safe, but they too are disgraced eventually under one pretext or the other. The ordinary employee is in fear every moment he or she labors there. A former Store Manager in Oklahoma said; "Those millions of workers there must rise up, and legally deal a crushing blow to the corrupt and criminal management of Walmart, and finally bring this 'citadel of slavery' to its knees."

In China, slavery is state sponsored, solely by the government and for the government. The number of individuals per capita involved in slavery in China is less in comparison to India, Pakistan, Bangladesh and other countries of the world. The Communist Party is the all-powerful and the almighty body, which decides every aspect of a human life: a form of a joint rule by the so-called proletariat against the common people.

In China, there is no such subject as Slavery, but there is an abundance in the supply of forced labor within the confines of a prison wall and within State managed farms and industrial units. This unambiguously translates into Slavery by the masses for the masses, by the workers against the workers! Thousand of such units lie scattered in that country, which has a land mass of 9,671, 018 square kilometers (approximately 3.7 million square miles) with a population exceeding 1.3 billion people and unfailingly growing by the hour.

In mid 1995 thousands of ethnic Uyghur people managed to flee China from brutality and repression, first for being Muslims and second for aspiring a separate State; the "Uyghur Republic." Escapees took with them documents and pictures purportedly reflecting the Chinese Government as brutal. Reports prepared by those who escaped claimed that The

Secretary General of the Communist Party of the People's Republic of China, the President and the Prime Minister are mere figureheads whereas the ruling elite and the lawmakers were nestled far away from the public eye.

Hundreds of thousands of Uyghur people have been kidnapped from their homes, shackled and transported by specially designed railway wagons to far off regions in the East to labor in State owned industrial complexes, including textile mills, steel plants, refineries, brick-kilns, mines, stone and mineral quarries and even pharmaceutical plants; almost everywhere and in any industrial unit. Their children, from infants to adolescents are in many cases sent to special camps to ensure a continued Communist majority in the country for the future. However, the mentally and physically disabled are also sent to labor in camps requiring non-specialized labor; brick kilns, farms and pig farms. Most of them are forced to work for eighteen hours a day. Several children have lost their lives due to cruel beatings if caught escaping.

The children, in case they are sent to join their parents, arrive in the same camp where their parents have been sent. All have a prominent tag on them for identification purpose. "They (the children) are treated like baggage which has to be sorted by their weeping parents." said Navid, a school teacher from the Uyghur region who had sought asylum in the USA.

The adults are sent to plants requiring more strenuous labor, sometimes to work for eighteen hours a day. Both the adults and children are plagued by disease because of malnourishment. Though provided medical care, a good number of them die to be cremated in the crematoriums on the property for this purpose! Grim faced guards who rarely speak but make stern gestures and motions order the other laborers to dump the body in an open flat bed truck. On several occasions, more than five people die in a day in any given industrial or farm complex while struggling to work.

"The trucks rarely come for a single body! Knowing fully well that on that day three or more will die from a workforce of a thousand workers, the trucks are not instructed to haul that single body. They know that more will die," said Liu Paul, a Christian preacher, once detained in a labor camp.

It is widely known that senior guards know the medical records of the detainees. They place the single dead body on the side of the work area and pile the other ones that die during the day on each other for late night when the slave laborers are free to stop work. The guards later load the dead bodies into trucks for cremation.

Children as old as six and seven are forced to work. This is State-sponsored slavery! Compared to individually sponsored slavery in India, the Chinese officials make feeble attempts to provide medical needs to a good percentage of these slaves but not out of generosity but due to time factors since replacing dead experienced hands means a slow-down in production rate.

Several unofficial and even unconfirmed sources claim that China has constructed most of its major projects like roads, bridges, dams, agricultural and industrial units through slave labor. At any given time, the government can mobilize some ten to fifteen million able-bodied individuals from its several camps to slave in its labor-intensive projects throughout the country. Almost a million of these people are ostensibly hired by the transportation system of the country, which includes shipping, railroad and highways. Another million are forced to work for the department of fisheries and another million for the department of agriculture and forestry. These are the labor arm of the departments with no pay but a little more than a bowl of fish soup and rice.

The most conservative number of State created slaves including those enslaved by the common citizenry in various forms can be put at twenty-five to thirty million! The accurate figure may never be known.

Reports claiming that most of the materials exported to Europe, Asia and the USA have been manufactured by trained slave labor have not been investigated in the least. As long as products from China at a very base price fulfill most of the needs of that particular country, investigators and reporters are hesitant to arouse the ire of their own government.

It is a challenge to prepare a complete report on the situation of the millions enslaved in China at the will and wish of the Chinese ruling hierarchy. The identity of the hierarchy's members is shrouded in total mystery. No particular individual can ever be approached for an explanation. The Chinese government does not take the trouble to answer to hundreds of letters and inquiries every day. The inquirer finally ceases to write!

Slave labor earns the Chinese Government tens of billions of dollars in foreign currency each year. So long as the treasury of the Chinese Government is overflowing with convertible currencies, and as long as prices of Chinese goods are low, no global Organization or Society will ever care to criticize China and its flagrant violation of Human Rights.

Even those countries claiming to husband the cause of Human Rights choose to adopt a struthious philosophy when it comes to China and cheap Chinese products.

The Chinese have a marked degree of success in their response to all these accusations and criticism if any. They never respond.

Pakistan

> "And who is responsible for this appalling child slavery? Everyone."
>
> Mother Mary H. Jones

This section of the book is dedicated to the memory of Iqbal Masih (1982-1995) a young Pakistani Christian who was forced into bonded labor in a carpet factory at the age of four, after being sold, became an international figurehead for the Bonded Labor Liberation Front at the age of ten after his daring escape from slavery and shot dead at the age of twelve.

An impoverished and an overpopulated country, Pakistan is a source, transit and a thriving place for various forms of crime by mankind against mankind; from child kidnapping to its final goal; slavery! Girls are primarily trafficked into Pakistan, mainly from Bangladesh, Iranian

Province of Baluchistan, Afghanistan, Myanmar, Nepal and Central Asia. Girls are trafficked for commercial sexual exploitation, exploitive labor and domestic slavery. A good number of them are trafficked to Arab Sheikhdoms in the Persian Gulf States of Kuwait, Bahrain, and Oman and in particular the UAE.

The US State Department in its report dated June 2009 claimed that the country's largest human trafficking problem is that of bonded labor, which is concentrated in Sindh and Punjab provinces, particularly in brick kilns, carpet-making, agriculture, fishing, mining, leather tanning and production of glass bangles. "Estimates of Pakistani victims of bonded labor, including men, women and children, vary widely but are likely over one million," the report said.

In mid 2012, a UN official at the United Nations in Geneva claimed that the statements and reports of the US State Department are incorrect and downplayed for obvious political reasons. There are at lest five million slaves of various descriptions in Pakistan with an area of virtually 800,000 square kilometers (307,374 square miles) and with a population fast approaching 180 million. This figure of slaves does not include another one million young girls sold by their parents into domestic servitude, prostitution or forced marriage as payment for debts.

Prominent Scottish Socialist Voice, Alan McCombes, in late 2001 stated that his research unearthed horrifying details of slavery in Pakistan. Poor families who received loans from any feudal employer, usually a brick kiln owner, a farm owner or a carpet manufacturer, had their entire family turned into the private property of the employer! Until the loan was repaid, the entire family was held in slavery.

The Human Rights Watch Asia stated in 1995 that millions of workers in Pakistan are held in contemporary forms of slavery. Employers forcibly extract labor from adults and children, restrict their freedom of movement and deny them the rights to negotiate the terms of their employment.

It is a fact that employers coerce such workers into servitude through physical abuse and forced confinement. Although slavery is unconstitutional in Pakistan and violates various national and international laws, state practices, support its existence. Fifteen years later in 2010, a spokesperson for Human Rights Watch Asia requesting anonymity claimed that at the present, confidential reports spoke about at least ten million slaves of various definitions exist in Pakistan. This translates into more than 5 percent of the entire population of the country to be in various forms of slavery. In early 2014, the figure reportedly exceeded ten million.

Hundreds of children employed in slave labor, dismantle condemned ships around the port city of Karachi. Many thousands are forced to collect metal scraps, glass bottles, aluminum cans and all forms of recyclable garbage in streets. "No individual is either properly paid, fed or receive any medical care. They are enslaved as soon as they are able to move an object, perhaps at the age of five. They die prematurely without any of their family members ever knowing their fate and future," said Saeeda Begum a Social Worker from Karachi.

Mrs. Begum, the wife of a retired army colonel blamed the rich landlords mostly from Karachi and Lahore who are actively involved in the destruction of these young lives, not caring to know that among them could be one day a very successful engineer, a surgeon or a physicist. In early 2013, she made a short speech at the famed Bolton Market in Karachi. She vociferously denounced every individual involved in this trade as contrary to all religious and moral ethics.

Speaking on the subject of those involved in slavery and the role of the rich in continuing it, she added, "All they care is money for themselves and their future generation. They have large tracts of land in the Punjab, Baluchistan and Sindh provinces. They are everywhere; just like an octopus, their gang strangles the very fabric of our society."

"Lives of the poor people have no value in the least for the rich property owners in Pakistan. These are the same rich people who have a free hand in expanding slavery in the country," said Bashir Khan a retired lecturer.

Pervez Musharraf, Army strongman of Pakistan (1999-2001 and later President until 2008) in early 2004 made the issue of eradication of slavery in Pakistan one of his cardinal programs. He had confided to his very close aide that this is his "War against Slavery in Pakistan" and had said that he would mobilize the entire armed forces of Pakistan in arriving at that goal. "I will wage a total war against this evil; I will personally lead the forces both from the Presidential office as well as in the cities, towns and villages. I will ask the entire nation to join me in this war against the enslavers. I will make them pay for exploiting mankind."

In 2008, the President was ousted through the money of the same enslavers who thought of him as encroaching on their business. The agitators in the various cities of Lahore, Karachi and Islamabad were the virtual slaves of these rich property owners said a prominent Pakistani journalist residing in the USA.

According to plans revealed by a senior retired army officer, a six months survey would reveal the names of those who formed the core of human trafficking and slavery throughout Pakistan. Elite members of the Pakistani armed forces would mount a sudden raid arresting hundreds of these dealers in human bondage and their lieutenants, all of whom afforded to have a private army guarding them and their luxurious residences in various parts of the country.

In early October 2007, President Pervez Musharraf had said to one of his most trusted military aide: "I will crush them and their trade and their corrupt lifestyle. If Pakistan has to be freed from this ugly label, if Pakistan has to come out of this shame, I will contribute my humble share. Those who will fight with me shoulder-to-shoulder will be those whose names will be eternally honored. I am just a servitor to Pakistan and its people. Enslavers are worst than any murderer. They are mass murderers. They go village-by-village, township by township and settlement by settlement picking their victims. The moment their victim is identified and taken, that victim's life is over. For several years, I was tied in the security of Pakistan, vis-à-vis external emergencies. We have good neighborly relations with India and our relations with Iran have been and will always be brotherly. Afghanistan is being handled with prudence and care. But now I can concentrate to tame this danger."

Ten months later on August 18, 2008, President Musharraf was forced to resign as the President of Pakistan.

However acute and exigent the situation of slavery in all forms may be in present day Pakistan, the government has not allocated time or resources to combat slavery. Neither there are any programs for the immediate future.

United Arab Emirates

> "Money is a new form of slavery, and distinguishable from the old simply by the fact that it is impersonal—that there is no human relation between master and slave."
>
> Leo Nikolayevich Tolstoy

For most of the unaware world Dubai in the United Arab Emirates, offers a place "far from the madding crowd!" It is not so, it is neither calm nor it has a good climate. Most important of all it does not have a benign form of government.

Dubai: Land of Luxury, Land of Slavery.

> "By investing in Dubai, celebrities are giving tacit approval to a hideous society and its obscene values."
>
> George Patrick

Dubai has officially banned slavery and prostitution in the 1960's, although the exact date remains unknown. Most recently, as early as the year 2000, in dozens of brothels, thousands of young women from Eastern Europe, South Asia, and Sub-Saharan Africa are held as sex slaves.

In his book, *A Crime So Monstrous*, journalist E. Benjamin Skinner points out that his $16 ticket to get into the Cyclone brothel actually bore the official stamp of the Dubai Department of Tourism and Commerce.

Skinner interviewed many of the prostitutes, some of them in their early teens. Most of them, seeking to escape desperate poverty in their homelands, volunteer to be smuggled into Dubai with the promise of jobs as maidservants, receptionists, telephone operators and companions for the elderly. The traffickers keep their passports or any identity papers.

Foreign laborers, mostly from the Indian subcontinent, if not exactly enslaved, receive a meager salary. The topic of child slaves in Dubai is a topic of global concern. Young boys often stunted in growth live in so-called farms often held in bondage to serve as jockeys in the popular Arab sport of camel racing. Human Rights report claims they are underfed to keep their weights low! Almost all are from Bangladesh, Pakistan and India.

Barely a week after these brutalities in Dubai was exposed by several independent journalists to the general public and the world in early 2004, more than half a million copies of this article was printed and openly handed over to the public in broad daylight. The President of the Emirates felt the anger of the public and first attempted to silence them but having failed stealthily asked his family members to find ways and means to put an end to this unrest. He thought that any increase in the anger of the public would be dangerous.

Initial plans called for asking Hosni Mubarak, President of Egypt to help them by sending Egyptian troops dressed as members of the armed forces of the Emirates. Wisdom told them otherwise. Thousands of foreign workers were arrested and imprisoned in makeshift holding areas. Hundreds who were seen distributing these articles were immediately arrested and some severely punished. The foreigners were immediately expelled without being paid for their works already performed; but not before being subjected to severe beatings. Many United Arab Emirate nationals were expelled from Dubai proper and placed on lists categorizing them as enemies of the State, God and the President of the United Arab Emirates, Khalifa bin Zayed Al Nahyan and Mohammad bin Rashid al Maktoum the ruler of Dubai, and their family members.

From then henceforth, the Al Nahyan and the Al Maktoum families became the most hated among the freedom loving people in the Arab World.

Several other documented articles appeared mysteriously, some mailed to the two ruling families listing their crimes against humanity, all the edicts of recognized religions and beliefs, and any norm of human decency.

V.M. Baskaran, a south Indian construction Engineer working with a construction company in Dubai accused the Officials of the United Arab Emirates as grossly wicked and anti-human. In a lengthy letter addressed to the Secretary General of the United Nations, Ban Ki Moon, Baskaran blasted the ruling Maktoum family of Dubai for their collusion with the President of the United Arab Emirates Khalifa bin Zayed for running a snake pit of slavery in Dubai and the surrounding regions of the UAE.

In his letter, V.M. Baskaran wrote; "Let not their combined wealth of nearly a hundred billion dollars and their claims of philanthropy detract you with their promises. They have only helped themselves and their crime ridden family members if at all. Khalifa bin Zayed al Nahyan is a known debauchee. His philanthropies and charities have never reached the really poor and struggling people of the world. Instead, the individual who is unworthy of calling himself an Arab ruler has spent hundreds of millions building himself a luxurious palace around the Island of Seychelles for his several concubines and mistresses. He is a known womanizer and corrupted to the bone. Arabs do not indulge in such hideous deeds. He (Nahyan) has approved one of the vilest things a human being could do; to simply order the cremation of those construction workers who either die in an accident while at work or ill, as if they have never lived, to save money paid by Insurance Companies either fully or partially owned by his family members. The Maktoum family is equally culpable for mistreatment of mankind, not only when alive but also after their demise. The majority of the workers, whether from India, Pakistan and Bangladesh are Muslims and rarely do they cremate. The immediate kin's of the dead are never contacted or informed. As for the ruling hierarchy of the United Arab Emirates, the dead never lived!"

A London based Organization supporting the cause of the workers throughout the Emirates claimed that in late 2009 thousands of unpaid workers in and around Dubai began to protest the way that they were treated and unpaid for months. Mass expulsions followed and by the end of 2010, more than twenty thousand foreign laborers were expelled from Dubai and another fifteen thousand from other parts of the Emirates. Almost all were from the Subcontinent. Most were given a one-way ticket to their country of origin. They were only allowed to take a few personal belongings, among them a few shirts, trousers and undergarments. An extra pair of shoes was also allowed. At the airport, they were each given a US ten dollar bill, courtesy of the two ruling families, the Al Maktoun and the Al Nahyan.

George Patrick, the Canadian freelance journalist and opinion writer claimed that he had exposed cruelty, slavery, and tyranny that are still masquerading as some sort of a benign rule by a joint rule of two Arab Caliphs in the United Arab Emirates. In his opinion column, he wrote, "In the twenty first century, these two Arab families have been exploiting mankind to their benefit in the most nefarious manner with no compassion or pity for the suffering common human being."

The two Arab families ruling in the United Arab Emirates have always presented themselves as a modern day "Robin Hood" by involving themselves in charities and philanthropies, to whitewash their corrupt and murderous lifestyles but with little success in the eyes of their fellow citizens whom they supposedly administer and care for. A few corrupt Institutes in Europe and the USA including a few Arab countries may have received some financial help, but only to build playgrounds, indoor swimming pools and libraries to be named after them, and other projects useless to the need of the common struggling person.

All said and thus written, a closer scrutiny of developments in the Emirates has created concern among the global community, albeit the millions and even billions of money pumped into the bank accounts and pockets of unscrupulous politicians in several major countries who have some sort of a political clout at International level. The job of the politicians of various countries is to continue to praise the United Arab Emirates as one of the most modernizing and humane societies in the

49

world under the direct auspices of the Al Nahayan and the Al Maktoum families. Further statements, perhaps throws more light on the plight of the common laborer and domestic servants turned into slaves by these Arabs Presidents, Emirs, Sultans and Sheikhs.

Reports stated that those very closely related to the ruling Al Nahyan family often place order to several suppliers as if the girls are commodities and that they should be between nine and twelve at the most. Khalifeh bin Zayed bin Sultan the ruler and President of the United Arab Emirates claims absolute immunity from any or all forms of criticism since his post and position provides him divine permission to satisfy his lust however he prefers. His younger brother, Abdullah bin Zayed al Nahyan who is also the Foreign Minister of the UAE has more than a dozen villas in several European countries where he keeps a harem of several dozen women from eight European Countries. "There is not the least concept of responsibility; not even in the faintest vein, where a dozen or so brothers and family members of the Nahyan family openly indulge in slavery, debauchery and domination," said Rifa Zvavi, an Omani businessman in Egypt.

Johann Hari wrote a lengthy article in "The Independent" on April 7, 2009 titled: "The Dark Side of Dubai," in which he presents a very grim and ominous picture of what he calls the "real" Dubai. He speaks of appalling conditions of the foreign workers, mostly from India, Pakistan and Bangladesh who have built Dubai to how it appears today. "They labor like slaves, are provided a meager ration to eat as slaves, live like slaves in shanty dwellings provided by the ruling family and die as slaves."

What is worse is that they are paid a very paltry amount. The government run media praise the Nahyan and the Maktoum family (who practically own the whole region) as those who built Dubai.

With an area of nearly 83,000 square kilometers (app. 32,000 square miles) and with a population of nearly eight and half million, the UAE is said to house a staggering figure of nearly a million slaves, of which at least fifty thousand are very young girls sexually exploited by the prominent members of the Al Nahyan family. Other Arabs of the Sheikhdom hold another two hundred thousand young women in bondage. The rest are indentured slaves. Nearly all are foreigners. The majority of the girl-slaves are from Morocco, Egypt, Tunisia, Libya, Bangladesh, Pakistan, India, Sri Lanka, Malaysia, Nepal and Afghanistan, while the men are from Pakistan, India, Bangladesh, and Sri Lanka.

Posterity will further prove the claimed benignancy or otherwise of the hierarchy in the United Arab Emirates.

Saudi Arabia

> "If there is a God, atheism must seem to Him a less of an insult than religion."
>
> Edmond de Goncourt

One may have repeatedly and regularly read news that in Saudi Arabia, a very close ally of the USA, a certain woman has been beheaded for having extra-marital relations or that a certain individual has had his or her limbs amputated for crimes deemed contrary to the tenets of the "Wahabi School of Thoughts" or that a person was simply beaten to death for insulting the King or any member of the Saudi Royal family! All such harsh and cruel punishments are condoned by the Kingdom's religious edicts, the laws laid by Wahabi sect clergymen. This sect created in the late eighteenth century became the official sect of Islam practiced by the majority in Saudi Arabia in early nineteenth century.

Members of the Saudi royal family number in thousands and nearly all of them are born immune to any form of legal proceedings against them by the common Saudi citizen. It is their birthright. They are above the law, since the laws are prescribed for the ordinary people and not members of the royal family who are only chosen to rule.

On May 14, 2012, a Nepali Watchdog reported that approximately 1300 people exit Nepal everyday, for work in the Arab Sheikhdoms of Kuwait, the United Arab Emirates, Bahrain and the Kingdom of Saudi Arabia. This also includes girls as young as twelve brought in to work as domestic servants for the Arabs. The larger percentage however is trafficked to Saudi Arabia. In November 2013, the Watchdog said that the figure had jumped to 1800 a day!

The document titled; "Human Trafficking and modern-day Slavery," states, "Saudi Arabia is named as a destination country for men and women trafficked for the purposes of involuntary servitude and, to a lesser extent, commercial sexual exploitation."

Men and women from Bangladesh, India, Sri Lanka, Nepal, Pakistan, the Philippines, Indonesia, Sudan, Ethiopia and many other countries voluntarily travel to Saudi Arabia as domestic servants or other low skilled laborers, but some subsequently face conditions indicative of involuntary servitude, including restrictions on movement, withholding of passports, threats, physical or sexual abuse, and non-payment of wages.

Human Rights groups in India and North African countries claim the existence of outright slavery and practices where young girls from India, Nepal, Afghanistan and several African countries, including, Sudan, Morocco, Algeria, Egypt and Tunisia have been escorted into Saudi Arabia by professionals; some of whom work for members of the Saudi Royal family. These professionals buy girls as young as seven years old from their parents, especially in Egypt, Morocco and Algeria with the promise of an immediate marriage with one of the so-called Princes.

Independent reporters and investigators have verified the claims of the popularly read document "Human Trafficking and Modern-day Slavery" which reported, "Some Saudi men have also legally contracted 'temporary marriages' in countries such as Mauritania, Yemen and Indonesia. The most sexually exploited are migrant workers."

Females as young as seven years old are led to believe they are being wed in earnest, but upon arrival in Saudi Arabia subsequently become the Arab's sexual slave and are forced into domestic work and, in some cases prostitution.

In the case of young girls and boys from Nepal, adults also go there for various forms of employment. Tragedy is the end result for most of these people. Dead bodies arrive back at an average of one every day in Nepal. That relates to those officially recorded as leaving Nepal to work in Saudi Arabia. Saudi officials categorize migrant workers as the ones coming from their own country but not those via a third country. Those coming directly from their own countries are carefully documented in the event of questions being asked in case of their demise or if they are missing.

"Several thousand cases have been recorded where bodies are simply cremated with their work clothes and their cheap bangles and imitation jewelry still on them. Their dead bodies are abused as much as when they were alive. In India, the case is five times when compared to dead bodies arriving back to Nepal; an average of five dead bodies return every day, but it has been insisted that at least twice that figure die every day due to torture, beatings, malnourishment and even killings by the employer. A similar scenario is in Pakistan, Bangladesh and Indonesia. An average of four to five bodies arrive in each of these countries every day," said a report from the office of an Indian Society, which rescues Nepalese, Indian and Sri Lankan slaves from Saudi Arabia.

Where Egypt, Morocco, Mauritania, Yemen and Algeria are related, the situation is simply horrible, just too horrible to even imagine. Social workers in both North Africa and South West Europe claim that since the past fifty years or so, the situation in these five Arab countries has been closely monitored; that young girls and boys are smuggled to Saudi Arabia for the pleasures of the Saudi Royal family and other rich people related to them.

Girls and boys as young as seven have been and are currently smuggled to Saudi Arabia on a regular basis. Since the children are brought in by doctored documents and the Saudi agent is usually the supposed uncle taking the child to his or her parent's residence in Saudi Arabia, there are no traceable documents for the child in case he or she is a victim to violence or meets a tragic end.

A watchdog group in Mumbai, India, requesting anonymity claims that members of the Saudi Royal family have presented each other with young girls from North African, South Asian and South East Asian Countries as an age-old practice.

The horrors meted out to foreign workers and migrants who are enslaved the minute they set foot on Saudi soil are neither an imagination nor a concoction or a falsification of the facts. No ulterior motive lies in demeaning the House of Saud. It is just a description of what they do.

Brian Evans, a popular investigative reporter wrote an article under the heading "The Plight of Foreign Workers in Saudi Arabia" in which he narrated an open case of slavery and bondage. The article states: "In November 1998 two Egyptian servants of Saudi Prince Turki bin Abd al-Aziz tied bed sheets together and lowered themselves from the rooms on the twenty ninth floor of the Ramses Hilton in Cairo where they had been imprisoned." They had been unpaid for months by the Prince.

The prince, a full brother of King Fahd, has lived for sixteen years on two floors of the five-star Cairo Hotel since his expulsion from Saudi Arabia for embarrassing behavior.

Research and investigation has shown that Prince Turki II was firmly asked to leave the Kingdom personally by the King due to his marital situation. On several occasions, the Prince warned the Saudi Royal family to leave the Kingdom and hand over power to the general public warning them of ominous developments to follow, just as in Iraq and Iran.

"We are presently witnessing the movement of the enraged public in Iran in quest of freedom from the hated and murderous clerical regime. The theocracy there is just a ploy to cling onto their shaky power by evil beings masquerading as clergyman and to hold the entire nation in chains and fetters. The regime there will fall and will fall, sooner or later, and so will the Saudi regime," the Prince warned.

Prince Turki II has never explained his own shortcomings in life of enslaving Egyptian workers and his parsimonious behavior. He has also refused to release any statement when repeatedly asked about the people he held in his various apartments in the Hotel. He has dismissed all the allegations as lies perpetrated by none but those among the members of the Royal Family who have their personal reasons of vendetta against him.

Sherman H. Skolnick, an investigative reporter in a document dated March 22, 2003 titled; "The Overthrow of the American Republic-Part 30," claimed a unit of the United Nations had documented a terrible truth that Saudi Arabia and Kuwait, according to details of the U.N., each had huge numbers of "Black Chattel Slaves" reminiscent of blacks in slavery.

According to the findings, the Saudis had one hundred thousand such slaves and Kuwait, about fifty thousand. Kuwait and Saudi Arabia are close allies of the United States of America.

The shocking figure of African slaves in Saudi Arabia does not limit the figure of slaves to one hundred thousand slaves. There are more than a million other slaves in many other forms and appearances. A good number are from the African Continent and from a dozen or more countries throughout Asia. Many die prematurely at the hands of their masters. The number of slaves in Saudi Arabia alone numbers around two hundred thousand. In Kuwait, it is at least one hundred thousand, including fifty thousand from Africa. Figures of people in bondage change every day.

A member of the United Nations' department of Human Rights requesting anonymity claimed that the figure in Saudi Arabia exceeds a staggering and mind shattering two million! Some Sheikhs are known to have fifty and even a hundred slaves. Members of the Saudi Royal family even openly boast and discuss among themselves the number of slaves they have and often discuss their plans of importing young girls from India and Nepal as young as seven. Some even claim a service to god, in that they convert the young virgin girls to their sect of Islam before they assault the human dignity of that girl.

Feroz Khan, the untiring movie star of India prepared a daring report for the United Nations in early 2006 reflecting the urgent need for the United Nations to set up a department with dedicated employees to combat the evils of slavery throughout the world, especially in the Arab countries, which is uncontrollably increasing. The report was promptly returned back to him a few weeks later with a covering letter claiming that there was no department in the United Nations. "No such department exists to address your claims and complaints. We have been receiving so many letters that we have no other alternative but to send it back to the sender," the letter from the United Nations stated.

Susan Taylor Martin writing in the St. Petersburg Times claimed that her investigation for the last ten years, since the year 2000 has unearthed massive human bondage and slavery in Saudi Arabia. In the year 2002, more than 2800 Sri Lankan housemaids ran away from their Saudi sponsors, claiming that they had been overworked, sexually abused and physically mistreated and held in slavery.

In 2007, it was reported that nearly three thousand women, mostly young girls were smuggled into Saudi Arabia from Indonesia and Bangladesh. Another four thousand were from India, Nepal and Pakistan in the same year. The figures from North African countries were not available due to reasons of fright from Saudi officials.

In 2009, it was stated that nearly two thousand women of various ages had managed to escape the misery by pretending to meet family members back home. It appeared that the girls and women orchestrated this excuse months earlier in a joint plan to leave the Kingdom. All had promised to return within weeks!

The Arab employer is never questioned in the Kingdom of Saudi Arabia concerning the death of a foreign worker. There are no laws requiring him to make any statement. He simply informs the police that a certain domestic servant or a laborer has just lost his or her life. The rest is taken care of. The reasons are very simple. Either he is a member of the Royal Saudi family or that he knows someone in that family or he is distantly related to any one of them through marriage. There are well over forty thousand members of the Saudi Royal family and another similar figure distantly related to them. Simple mathematics conveys the hidden message.

Kuwait, Saudi Arabia, United Arab Emirates and Bahrain have been singled out as the worst offenders where Human Rights are concerned. The Saudis consider any person working or toiling for them as those who are condemned by destiny; be it a laborer, a technician, an engineer or even a surgeon from another country. They view the US Servicemen on their land as mere workers fit to die for them in case of a crisis or an emergency. They consider the British and the French as a curse of creation. They rarely thank any individual for any help or service rendered.

Saudi Arabia is a country with an area of 2,250,000 square kilometers (870,000 square miles) and with a population of nearly 30 million people.

This Kingdom has a few industries not worthy of mention, houses more than one and half million slaves, perhaps a million of them living in the most shocking and appalling condition. There is not a single globally Organized Society to confront the massive crime against humanity in Saudi Arabia

It was Dr. Kurt Herndl, the fourth leader of the Center for Human Rights at the United Nations in Geneva, 1982-1987, who spoke his mind about outright slavery in Arab countries. His relentless labors led to the establishment of UN special "Rapporteur" against torture. He was the first to be designated "Assistant Secretary General for Human Rights." In mid 1986 Dr. Herndl, a fiercely incorruptible man, warned that several countries are openly practicing slavery under the guise of permissible religious edicts vis-à-vis their workers and in a private meeting singled the United Arab Emirates, Saudi Arabia, Bahrain and Kuwait as the worst of the worst offenders.

In 1987, Dr. Herndl was confidentially asked to tender his resignation! He quietly disappeared from the socio-political scene altogether.

Javier Perez de Cuellar y de la Guerra in 1988, the then Secretary General of the United Nations (1982-91) caved in to private meetings with the ambassadors of Saudi Arabia and Kuwait. The spastic Secretary General, who spoke halting French and English, that was barely audible, agreed to the need to have a special understanding and working relations with the Arab countries who regularly contribute more than their share to the United Nations' Special Fund. It was even reported that Perez de Cuellar had gone to the extent of repeatedly apologizing to the Saudi and Kuwait ambassadors for the inconveniences caused to their Kings, Emirs and Sheikhs. The proceeds of these funds are unknown to this day! How this money and for what purposes this money has been used so far is a mystery, but the amount is said to be in tens of millions every year.

His predecessor Mr. Kurt Josef Waldheim (Secretary General of the United nations 1971-81) however, was not only corrupt; he had walked with crime and corruption all his life. He had a shady past. It was a known fact, even before being elected as the Secretary General of the United Nations that he had a Nazi past! It was he who had ordered his close aides to disallow any form of statements to be made against the Saudi Royal family, the Al Maktoum, the Al Nahyan and the Kuwait Al Sabah family in any major United Nations meeting. In fact, he had employed a group of Egyptian nationals, well above the required Egyptian quota as his emergency prerogative for an important mission; to safeguard any form of attack on Kuwait, Saudi Arabia, United Arab Emirates including Dubai and Bahrain by unfriendly countries where slavery and Human Rights were concerned.

"While Perez de Cuellar was not a corrupt person, he was a very frightened man. I met him several times. He had a very nervous disposition and felt that the Saudis and the Kuwaitis could topple him anytime they wanted with their money. Waldheim on the other hand was a cold and a calculating individual with virtually no moral scruples. In essence, during his tenure in office, he had banned the subject of attacks on the two Arab heads of State, through his agents working as 'experts and advisers.' Once I mentioned to him the topic of slavery in Saudi Arabia and he felt startled. He claimed he had no such reports nor did he ever hear of such developments in that country," said Alexandre Hay, President of the International Committee of the Red Cross based in Geneva (1976-87).

Meanwhile rumors were intentionally floated within the United Nations that Herndl had asked to be relieved of his duties due to health reasons.

Although the practice of slavery was abolished in Saudi Arabia in 1962, it thrives today, on a higher scale.

Kuwait

> "Slavery is theft—theft of a life, theft of work, theft of any property or produce, theft even of the children a slave might have borne."
>
> Kevin Bales

It is of subtle importance to note that Kuwait with 3.6 million inhabitants living in 6880 square miles (17,820 square kilometers) is home to more than a quarter million people forced to live in enslavement!

Kuwait has been described as a destination country for men and women trafficked for the purposes of forced labor. The majority of them are among more than half a million foreign women recruited for domestic service work in Kuwait. They are chiefly from Bangladesh, Pakistan, Sri Lanka, Indonesia, India, Nepal and the Philippines.

A report claims that although they migrate willingly to Kuwait, upon arrival the sponsors subject them to various forms of brutalities. Employers take their passports and confine them in very small rooms. Almost every modern and large villa in Kuwait has a small "punishment room" for domestic servants who refuse to comply with any given order.

As early as 1995 it was reported in Human Rights Global Report that since late 1991 after the liberation of Kuwait from the temporary occupation of Iraq, more than two thousand women from various South and East Asian countries and a similar figure of young girls from Nepal have fled the homes of abusive employers. Almost all of them arriving at Delhi airport claimed to have been imprisoned in small rooms for days chained and even sexually abused.

Kuwait's labor laws exclude foreign workers from their labor law protection albeit the fact that Kuwait has since long depended on foreign workers to be the backbone of its labor. It is a known fact that Kuwait has more than fifty thousand black people, all virtually in open slavery! They are a reminiscent of slavery in the USA. Nearly ten people of African origin arrive each day in Kuwait accompanied by an agent who arranges their travel documents through instructions from the Emir's family members who pride themselves as having Africans as slaves in their pompous residence.

By the same token, an average of three to four people of African origin die every day, either due to disease, undernourishment, and even while being beaten! They are all cremated unannounced and without any records or any news in the press which is state owned. None, virtually none is ever paid since the philosophy is that these human beings are to be treated as chattels. They are condemned to die in Kuwait in bondage and in chains. They are rarely able to return to their homeland. This reminds one of slavery in the USA, where the slaves never returned to Africa. Hence, they

59

do not need any money, but a mere morsel of bread to keep them alive while they toil until their last days in the house of an Arab related to the Emir of Kuwait.

It has been a case study of the Al Sabah family with nearly four thousand members, that each family has at least five slaves of African origin, two "dignified" slaves of Egyptian nationality, one Algerian and at least twelve young girls, mostly from Morocco, Algeria and Nepal for the private pleasures of the already married cumbersome appearing "lesser Sheikhs." Another five thousand members of the extended Al Sabah family have the same number of slaves. Still another ten thousand affording Arab families have between two to five slaves with a few unspecified young girls serving the lusts of the rich Kuwaiti Arab. The girls cannot be properly accounted for since all are forced to wear veils.

"Kurt Waldheim, the most dubious Secretary General that the United Nations ever had, gave these rich rulers a guaranteed form of protection. I do not see much hope from the present administration of the United Nations, while his successor is doing the same," said Justice Whitaker of the USA, attending the Sub-Committee meeting on Human Rights and Slavery in Geneva, mid 1984.

At least half a dozen various Societies in the African Continent and a similar number in England, France and the Netherlands have concluded that there are at any given time more than one hundred thousand human beings either in invisible chains and fetters or bonded slavery in Kuwait.

The Anti-Slavery International based in England in early 2012 claimed that the figure was in the excess of one hundred thousand. Deaths, chiefly due to deprivation of food, beatings and punishments are the main factor of nearly a thousand per year. An African Society based in Senegal claimed more than a thousand five hundred black people alone die each year due to tortures and beatings linked to their enslavement in Arab countries. Once sick, they are transferred into a room ironically called "recovery room." There, they are left to die. There is no medical help of any kind, not even a pain-relieving tablet. Almost all luxury villas, belonging to the Kuwaiti Emir's extended family members have a "punishment" and a "recovery" room.

Alexandre Hay (then President of the International Red Cross) in early 1984 said: "I have been confidentially informed by my special assistant that rarely does any slave or those in bonded slavery ever recover or resuscitate from their illness when sick in Kuwait, Saudi Arabia, the Arab Emirates and Bahrain. A common practice among these members of the elite family in these countries is that they look down on humankind, especially the Africans, Indians, Nepalese and even their own brethren, the Egyptians and Algerians as being only fit to serve them until their last breath. No medical attention is ever provided and it has been suggested but not proved that some semi-conscious slaves are dumped into trucks to be taken to a privately owned crematorium outside the city limits. Unconfirmed reports claimed that many are still alive when shoved into crematorium's oven! This is shocking and appalling. Here we have odious scenes reminding us of death camps in Europe during the 30's and 40's. This could be the most evil crime if at all such a thing has ever taken place. And, by all measures I stand to honor the report of my Special Assistant."

Whether the disease of slavery is rampant in Kuwait or is only limited to members of the Al Sabah family practicing it, there is ample indication of the existence of slavery in that Sheikhdom. Similar to the horrifying cases in Saudi Arabia, the United Arab Emirates, Dubai included, and Bahrain, it appears that there is a consistent and a uniform trend in addressing the slaves as "them." Keeping "them," using "them" and finally disposing "them" is a common code term used among the elites of the Al Sabah family.

In his life and death, the slave is without papers and identities save for a doctored document provided by unscrupulous agents for the purpose of entry into those Sheikhdoms and Emirates. While alive, the individual is doomed to live in a cocoon of perpetual misery; misery created by rich and affording human beings not caring to value life and living. In death, the victim does not even qualify as a statistic.

The "Dr Jekyll and Mr. Hyde" tactics of the Saudi, Kuwaiti, Bahraini and the Emirates' government at the International Organizations continues. The Emirs, Sheikhs, and Kings continue to play the role of concerned rulers only wishing the well-being of all.

Kingdom of Bahrain

> "Any unarmed people are slaves, or are subject to slavery at any given moment."
>
> Huey Newton

Bahrain is a destination country for men and women trafficked for the purposes of forced labor and commercial sexual exploitation. Agents of rich Arabs lure young girls and boys from Morocco, Egypt, Tunisia, India, Pakistan, Nepal, Sri Lanka, Bangladesh, Indonesia, Thailand, the Philippines, Ethiopia and Eritrea into Bahrain on promises of child-care and attractive salaries. Most of them upon arrival in Bahrain are immediately turned into sex-slaves.

Bahrain, the United Arab Emirates, Kuwait and Saudi Arabia are among the close allies of the United States of America. These countries in particular have rarely been challenged either at the United Nations or at any International Organization affiliated to the United Nations or the United States of America concerning the open acts of slavery practiced in their country; especially by members of the ruling family and in many cases the rulers themselves.

The enslavers are not entirely Arabs from Bahrain. They are originally businessmen from Qatar, Doha, Sharjah, Ajman and Abu Dhabi but who own luxury homes in Bahrain ostensibly to have extra-marital sex slaves, far from the eyes of their family members.

Unlike the rulers and family members of Saudi Arabia, United Arab Emirates, Dubai and Kuwait, neither the ruler of Bahrain nor any member of his family are involved in slavery either through labor or for the exploitation of underage girls. Investigations have however pointed to this fact that Bahrain has become a rest and recreation place for several members of the Saudi Royal family including a few of the Al Nahyan and Al Maktoum families.

In Bahrain, it is the common Arab citizen of that Island who attempt to imitate their other brethren in Saudi Arabia, United Arab Emirates, Kuwait and Dubai by having a few domestic servants; mostly young ladies and in some cases underage girls from Egypt, Indonesia, Pakistan, India, Sri Lanka and the Philippines.

U.S. Department of State Bureau of Democracy, Human Rights and Labor in a Memo published on March 6, 2005 stated that, Labor laws (in Bahrain) do not apply to domestic servants.

There were numerous credible reports that domestic servants, especially women, were forced to work 12 or 16 hours days, given little time off, were malnourished, and were subjected to verbal and physical abuse including sexual molestation and rape. Between 30 to 40 percent of the attempted suicide cases handled by the government's psychiatric hospitals were foreign maids. It was estimated that there were 50,000 foreign housemaids working in the country.

In May 2012, Bahrain's Labor Ministry reported that the entire population of the Island kingdom was 740,000, which included nearly 300,000 foreign workers. Included also was the new number of foreign housemaids which stood at 60,000. Often a Bahraini family had three or four housemaids.

In early 2013, Human Rights groups in India and Pakistan said that the number of foreign housemaids living in slavery in Bahrain constantly change due to several factors. In case they die of accidents, beatings, punishments or illness, and have no person as a contact either in their own country or elsewhere, their bodies are secretly disposed of. The employers usually take their passports the moment the housemaids arrive in Bahrain.

On August 7, 2006, the Bahraini Television reported a huge fire at the Gudaibiya Labor Camp where laborers worked in slave-like conditions, often whipped and in leg-irons! The television reporter claimed that human trafficking has been reported in that camp and investigations were underway. Initial reports stated that sixteen people had perished in the blaze. Later independent reports confirmed that more than twenty dead bodies of slaves were being burned to eradicate any trace of their existence. Independent journalists said that most of the dead were from the Sudan, India and Bangladesh.

Indian Ambassador Balkrishna Shetty had asked the Bahrain Foreign Ministry to investigate what he alleges were violations of international laws against human trafficking.

On August 11, 2006, the same scene had been fully cleaned and washed! Although no traces of human ashes were visible after the clean-up, for more than a month the area was closed to the general public. Repeated washing of the entire region changed the scene beyond any recognition.

On March 13, 2009, John Defterios reported one of the several cases of slave labor and even outright slavery in the Khaleej Times Online: "Forty year old Suryavathi Rao fled the home of her employer that morning shoeless with only a nightgown and a bible to her name." Reports circulated that the years of domestic labor have taken their toll. She could easily pass for 60 if not a few years older. After working sixteen hours a day, seven days a week for a year and half, Suryavathi could not take it anymore. She said through a translator that her meager salary of 108 US dollars had not been paid for six months. She complained about not being fed meals and surviving on the generosity of her neighbor, another domestic servant who pulled together leftovers to get by.

In the following year, in late 2010, Manama the capital witnessed several cases of suicide by very young Egyptian and Thai girls, some said to be as young as fourteen and fifteen. Virtually all of them were found to have doctored travel documents, which were later on presented to the authorities by the employers who kept these papers to prevent their escape. Bahraini authorities immediately cordoned off the whole streets while the bodies were being taken to a waiting unmarked truck instead of an ambulance and informed the public that it was a common case of family dispute!

In the "Pattaya Daily News," a daily publication from Thailand dated May 12, 2005, a strong warning was made to the Thai women and young girls not to be lured to Bahrain by false promises of well-paid jobs. "If you were convinced by someone who promised you a well-paid job in Bahrain, don't trust them. They will tell you of a dream-like city, what you'll face is like a hell," the article reported.

In spite of regular warnings and announcements in various newspapers in Thailand of the dangers facing migrant workers in Bahrain and other sheikhdoms, human traffickers lure young girls there through promises of a better life abroad. Chandra Bhumol identifying herself as a social worker in Bangkok claims to insert such announcements in minor newspapers in the small cities of Thailand.

"It is from these small villages in Thailand that most of the young girls are openly bought and sold and even kidnapped and 'shipped' to various Arab countries as if they were pots and pans. Without any exception all of the young girls are turned into slaves as soon as they set foot on any of these Arab countries," she explained.

The victims do not speak any other language and can only cry and cry for the misery that befalls them. The common Arab has no pity. The worst part of it is that they are immediately converted to Islam by these thugs. They do not know what is happening. Their employer, or rather, their buyer and owner, has a ready made script in Thai but written in Arabic alphabets, which he reads loudly, informing her that henceforth she has such and such a name and will serve her new master in any way so as to please him and to obey him at all costs. The girl out of fright nods in affirmation! There is no recourse for them over there for their grievances; they have no office to hear their complaint just because most of their papers are doctored. Once over there, they feel a death sentence has been passed over them with their execution to follow any time.

All told, it is to be added that unlike the other Arab rulers and Emirs in the Persian Gulf, the ruling Al Khalifa family in Bahrain are less blamed but only responsible for not taking any active role to put an end to this trade which has reportedly taken more than five thousand lives in the last twenty years; lives of young girls bought into slavery and who died or were killed while in chains and fetters done by none but mankind.

Theocratic Islamic Republic of Iran

Iranians in exile vociferously say that as long as there is widespread superstition and no unity and determination, and until that moment there are soothsayers and yes-men surrounding the uneducated theocratic tyrant, enslavement of the nation will never end. The tyrant will continue to betray and hold the nation hostage, enslave and murder through decree, often calling it a will of the Omnipotent One. Once these barriers are overcome, the false scaffoldings of that ordinary human being in the garb of an ethereal figure will crash and be dismantled in a blinking of an eye.

> "Watch out for the fellow who talks about putting things in order! Putting things in order always means getting the people under your control."
>
> Denis Diderot

Ever since in February 1979 a clergy led revolution replaced the progressive and modernizing Shah of Iran, the country has undergone dramatic social changes, most of it for the worst. Radical laws and outdated religious tenets have pulverized the daily lives of the millions of Iranians, forcing nearly five million of the then thirty eight million people into exile.

Today, the Iranian population in exile has exceeded nine million with the majority preferring to live in Europe and elsewhere than in the U.S.A. or Canada.

The seat of power was grabbed by the clergy, the majority of them being "seyeds;" people of non-Iranian origin who claimed to be descendents of Mohammed, the prophet of Islam. They were and are in the minority; barely 3 percent of the seventy six million people, but they hold a powerful grip over the entire country. If a clergy, they don the black turban. Clerics with white turban are of Iranian origin.

There is analogy between the Alawites holding power in Syria and the Seyeds ruling Iran. The former constitute a mere 12 percent of the population; some one million of the thirteen million population whereas the latter; the Seyeds, constitute 3 percent of the entire population of nearly seventy six million people of Iran. Before seizing power, the Alawites in Syria were the poorest, and most despised. The same deals with the ethnic minority Seyeds in Iran who are the rulers of the country and who are now the most hated. Both follow the Shiite School of Thought in one form or the other.

However, a strange analogy exists between the two minorities ruling the majorities. In Syria, the Alawites are of Arab origin and are in an Arab country, whereas in Iran, the Seyeds are of Arab origin in a nation of Indo-Europeans.

In Iran, there is no slavery in the true meaning of the word like in Arab or south Asian and Far East Asian countries where human beings are bought, sold, and even bartered by the citizens. Some isolated cases have been however recorded in Iran since the past thirty years.

In Iran, another form of slavery exists, state-sponsored! In the past thirty years and more, tens of thousands of those deemed as enemies and potential enemies of the state or imagined to be those waging a war against god but in fact against the theocratic hierarchy, are arrested and sent to various camps spread throughout the country without any trial. There, the individual is made to toil; a reminder of slave labor extracted from Jews in the 30's and 40's in Germany. The enslaved political prisoner in the theocratic regime perishes without any trial or hearing. His average years in imprisonment performing slave labor is said to be between two and three years. He is condemned through the unwritten edicts of god, known only to the clergyman. His body is usually buried in a pit or, not to be outdone by other tyrants, is cremated without any formality.

"Iran Clergy Watch," a virtually unknown publication in a pamphlet distributed in Hamburg, Germany in February 2012 stated: "A group of attorneys who made an independent investigation into the situation of slave labor and other forms of slavery in Iran in early 2010 claimed that developments in the clergy run country is an affront to society and mankind."

The attorneys, eight from western European countries, two from Central Asian countries and two former attorneys who fled Iran forwarded their findings in early December of 2011 to the Human Rights Center at the United Nations in Geneva and the Anti Slavery Organization based in London. The Center in Geneva did acknowledge their report while the Organization in London responded that it is launching its own investigations.

"Iran Focus" reported on April 11, 2005 that a number of government officials and security officials were arrested in raids in at least five houses in and around the town of Neka (northern Iran). Those arrested were two clergymen and eleven senior members of the Revolutionary Guards of the clergy run regime. The raids conducted during two weeks uncovered several organized child prostitution rings and brothels where girls as young as twelve and thirteen were forced into prostitution. In addition to that, more than twenty children, some below ten were held against their will by senior members of the Revolutionary Guards who see themselves as belonging to the elite society in Iran. Residents in Neka said that there was a small graveyard behind one of the larger brothels. More than a dozen underage girls were rescued while in chains. Some were tied behind their backs and a dozen or more were imprisoned in a small room.

The place was once a thriving industrial plant manufacturing electrical parts for housing.

The property was confiscated in March 1980 by the clergy regime and dismantled since it belonged to a Baha'i businessman. The Baha'i family had operated this plant for the past quarter century employing at least a hundred people. Followers of the Baha'i Faith number more than half a million in Iran with more than six million followers throughout the world. They are the largest minority in the country and number more than all the minorities combined.

More than a month earlier in March, "Iran Focus" also reported that at least 54 Iranian girls and young women, between the ages of 16 and 25 were smuggled out of Iran and taken to Pakistan, where they were sold in the streets of Karachi. The tragedy is that such an atrocious act is committed daily in Karachi. The report further added that there were at least 300,000 runaway girls in Iran, adding that the estimated number of woman under the absolute poverty line was more than eight million. In 1987, the same source presented a very grave picture of the situation in which it stated that there are more than fifteen million women under the absolute poverty line in Iran.

There is no official document reflecting the number of slave labor employed by the theocracy in Tehran. Many in exile often quote exaggerated figures running into millions, sometimes five million. This appears to be a far-fetched figure. At the most, there may be fewer than a million human beings employed in slave labor. Their ages range from twelve to ninety, but this is a State-sponsored and managed slavery!

Considering the one hundred and fifteen known labor camps and the three hundred penitentiaries throughout the country housing nearly one and a half million imprisoned, one could better justify half a million or a lesser figure held in slave labor originally condemned as political prisoners. They form a 35 percent of all those incarcerated. Teenagers are also categorized as political prisoners if their parents were arrested as defaulters. In case a husband was arrested, his wife and children underwent the same procedure of a political prisoner and all had to spend the remainder days of their lives as slaves or till the day they were pardoned by the clergyman leader.

Of major importance is that all, regardless of their age and health, notwithstanding their crimes, they are defined as slaves and will remain slaves until they die. "They are the cursed and the condemned of the earth," according to the rulings of clergyman Khamenei.

After fully using their labors to the point of exhaustion for nearly sixteen hours a day, they were fed a piece of flat bread and some unwashed greens and vegetables from the large farms where they toiled. Once ailing, they were simply divided into two categories; worthy of being treated and if so, will his labors at least compensate his medical expenses if treated or if he is beyond extensive and specialized care.

Most shocking is that there is a uniform method of disposing the bodies of the victims in labor camps of the most unpopular regime; open fire pits for a few or crematoriums for a larger number.

One tends to remember words that will rest forever in infamy; those chilling words on the gates of Auschwitz death camp where millions of innocent human beings lost their precious lives; *"Arbeit Macht Frei;"* Work liberates, or rather, liberation of mankind through slave labor. Now, that is happening in the vast prison of a theocratic regime in Iran with Khamenei as the chief prison warden of the entire country. Instead of that mind-shattering slogan in German, the regime in Tehran has coined an unheard of phrase, insisting it is from the Koran claiming it means, "Allah loves workers," which is placed at the entrance of slave-labor camps. Nearly all the slave labor camps have their own crematoriums. They are ubiquitously present in every slave labor camp.

Private investigations of at least half a dozen known notorious labor camps in Karaj, Esfahan, Ahwaz, Shiraz, Kerman and Tehran, between the months of May and September 2011 revealed that the majority of the prisoners had died of exhaustion and dehydration while laboring on farms with heavy chains fettered to their ankles. Among the dead were eight young boys whose parents were arrested in late June 2009, immediately after the controversial June 12, 2009 presidential elections. They were transferred to Kerman and Esfahan provinces far away from Tehran. Distant family members of the deceased boys said that they were aware that the children of the imprisoned parents and immediate family members were imprisoned for participating in demonstrations against Ahmadinejad and the "dictator," a reference to clergyman Ali Khamenei. All worked on farms producing fresh vegetables.

Close family members said that they were too frightened to disclose the identities of their family members arrested to the reporters for fear of retribution. Those incarcerated were branded as co-sinners against Khamenei who also claims to be the representative of god on earth. Reports in early 2011 said that at least fifty prisoners died in the provinces of Esfahan and Kerman in one day. All died while still in chains. This news was reflected in pamphlets distributed in the cities of Esfahan, Kerman, Shiraz and Qom. In October 2012, reports circulated that the combined toll was over a hundred dead in a day in the Provinces of Lorestan, Fars, Kerman and Esfahan in the month of August of that year. Clergyman Khamenei the self-appointed Leader dismissed such figures of his opponents and claimed Islam ordained the deaths. In his usual monologue, he claimed a very negligible number of mischief mongers lost their lives while challenging the rule of god. Iranian mass media in exile uniformly reported that mass slaughter of the public was underway throughout the country with very few International Organizations protesting the regime's murderous deeds.

The accurate figure of premature deaths due to violence and slave labor in the Islamic Theocracy is a challenge to a common reporter and investigator. In 1999 distraught families who had not heard of their children's fate for four years reported more than a thousand deaths. Other prison inmates leaked the news through their own grapevine. Considering a figure of an average of one thousand people dead or killed through the excesses of slave labor each year, one could put the figure at an astonishing number of nearly thirty thousand murdered by the Islamic regime in the past thirty and odd years. This is not related to the thousands of political prisoners simply massacred in the last thirty years or so. Given the fact that at least a thousand die each year due to several factors including beatings, punishments and disease all arising out of forced labor in the harshest conditions, the regime must find ways to keep the number of workers constant, which means random imprisonment. At the same time, it must find means to keep the death of the unfortunate citizens a secret, which it fails.

"In 1991 clergyman Khamenei, already invested with the title of 'Leader' issued a religious edict claiming he had received divine orders asking him to categorize young girls and children; even infants as prisoners of the State if their parents commit any form of violation or acts against god's rule on earth! In the same year, the Revolutionary Guards snatched thousands of children, some of them three to four years old from their guardians or grandparents and taken to various prisons to atone for the sins of their parents who were already in prison and serving slave labor. Several hundreds died in the first ten months due to untreated illness they already had. Clergyman Khamenei had become a gangster, a mobster, and a ruthless killer, that too of children. He never uttered a word about their death which was known throughout the country and where the international mass media refused to even write a line about it," said Dr. E. Homayounfar a former Undersecretary of the Ministry of Information of the Imperial Government living in exile in Geneva in November 1992.

Dr. Homayounfar said that the most befitting quotation to describe the officious deeds of this regime would be from Shakespeare's "The Tempest." He quoted the lines: "Hell is empty and the devils are here!"

The U.S. Department of State for Human Rights Division in Early April of 2012 in an internal memo stated that eighteen reports prepared by various Societies and Organizations in Europe, the United States and Asia, about executions and slavery in Iran between the years 1980-2010 closely match each other. Reports reveal a staggering figure of those condemned to death and executed for crimes against the state and various other crimes at about one hundred and twenty thousand. Of these, nearly forty thousand executed in this period were members of the People's Mujaheddin Organization, a group that had once actively lent support to cleric Khomeini in his quest to oust the late Shah. The group and its leaders escaped the country. The clergy regime in Tehran considers them a terrorist group. The Iranian nation also despises that group and considers them as those responsible for Islamic revolution.

The report also stated that those who died while undergoing slave labor within the same period are estimated to have been twelve to fifteen thousand. All died within the confines of the labor camps.

Ali Khamenei, a formerly obscure and a half-literate clergyman is the present Leader of the Islamic Theocracy in Tehran. Although he has chosen to be addressed as the "Supreme Leader," he is also addressed as the "glorious leader" and many of his soothsayers address him as "The All Knowing, The All Wise," and many times as "The Peerless One" and even a Saint! Little information exists of his past except that he had indoctrination in the Soviet Union between the years 1965-68 and later underwent some militia training in terrorist-breeding camps managed by the Palestinians under Yasser Arafat. On his stay abroad, he thought it better to live under the garb of a clergyman for obvious reasons.

Both clergymen Khomeini, the individual credited by the West as having led a movement to unseat Monarchy in Iran and Khamenei, his successor, have no knowledge about their parents or their burial site. Until today, the identities of the parents of these two individuals have remained clouded.

Meanwhile, both these clerics have been embellished and parental identities created for them.

As a suspected troublemaker without any known trade or profession, Khamenei was a marked person and closely watched by the Security Services of the Imperial Police. Former officials of the Imperial Government rejected the false pretence of Khamenei as being in prison for his religious or anti-Shah beliefs. "He was a simple rabble-rouser, an opportunist and a part-time beggar, and he played his role well then and now," said Dr. E. Homayounfar.

Since being chosen by the previous leader (Khomeini) days before his death, Khamenei has never given a single interview to any newspaper or mass media in general. He has spoken in monologues, often invoking his spiritual prowess and his ethereal gift to communicate with god. For the past few years "The Peerless One," "The All Knowing, and The All Wise" is shown wearing a pink cloak, often reminding those around him that this was one of the commands of god to him!

In the majority of his monologues, the subject of enemies is always discussed. He threatens his tormentors and demeans those opposed to the clergy rule as enemies of god. He never alludes to friends. He constantly reminds the nation that those "crossing the line" would be severely dealt with and at intervals reminds the would-be-defaulters of laboring in the fields to feed the believers.

A correct picture of slavery in the Theocratic regime in Iran can never be accurately assessed. Emotionally charged statistics and hearsay would in no way serve the purpose of pinning the regime in any International Court of Justice. What is crystal clear is that there have been executions, tens of thousands, perhaps more than a hundred thousand with a substantial number of them perishing under slave labor in the past three and half decades.

Turkey

> "Human kind is made up of two sexes, women and men. Is it
> possible that a mass is improved by the improvement of only
> one part and the other part is ignored? Is it possible that if half
> of a mass is tied to earth with chains and the other half can
> soar into the skies?"
>
> Mustafa Kemal Ataturk

Turkey is a destination and simultaneously a transit country for women
and children predominantly from Eastern Europe and the former Soviet
Union trafficked for sexual exploitation as well as slave labor.

It has been noted that since the past forty-five years, women from the
Baltic countries are smuggled into Turkey, by boats, sometimes dozens
at a time. Nearly a thousand of them arrive each year through the
various unguarded borders of Turkey. In many cases, border guards are
bribed with a few US dollars. The guards do not care that they may be
even individuals among them under the guise of prostitutes who may
compromise the security of Turkey or may be on their way to NATO bases
inside Turkey to indulge in sabotage.

An appalling case was mentioned on November 5, 2004 by "Independent
Online News" where a young ten year old Tajik boy was abducted in
broad daylight near his school in Dushanbe and driven to a remote place
where he was transported into a light plane and flown to an airfield in
Afghanistan and from there to Turkey over the Caspian Sea and finally to
the United Arab Emirates. The boy's parents lodged a complaint through
the Tajik Ministry of Foreign Affairs since it was rumored that most of
the abductees are finally found in the various Sheikhdoms of the United
Arab Emirates. The authorities in the Emirates did not even respond to
the Tajik Foreign Ministry's official investigations. Tajik news sources
reported the vast majority of abductees are first trafficked to Turkey,
where the chief agent sorts out the boys according to the orders he has
received from the various Sheikhs.

A non-government agency operating in Turkey to prevent child abduction
for slavery in an Online Report dated April 12, 2012 claimed that it is

shocking to note that there are holding areas for children abducted mostly from the Balkans and the Commonwealth of Independent States. Another group calling itself "The Action Now" is based in a modest home in Istanbul. "We do not belong to any registered Society. Our main aim is to expose criminals who come to Turkey from Arab countries and have turned Istanbul as their trading center; center to trade human beings, auction them and sell them like automobiles or used furniture."

More shocking is that these groups peddling in slavery and human beings have their own guards and even henchmen to either kill or abduct and then dispose of the bodies of people suspected of interfering or investigating their criminal activities.

A non-governmental organization in Tajikistan said, "There was a growing trend in the abduction and sale of Tajik boys for sexual exploitation abroad." The "MODAR" organization, (A group working in the Tajik Republic to unite women and support their active participation in supporting peace and agreement in society), said groups in the United Arab Emirates, Turkey, Pakistan and Saudi Arabia were prepared to pay as much as seventy thousand U.S. dollars for a Tajik boy between the ages of ten and twelve. The Organization revealed in early 2012 that several of its members visited the United Arab Emirates as tourists while investigating the case of nearly two hundred young Tajik boys abducted and taken to the various Sheikhdoms of the United Arab Emirates between the years 2009 and 2010.

Armed with the missing children's picture and birth certificates, the group spent some two months travelling the Emirates with their personal guards posing as tourists like them. They managed to discover some grizzly facts that eight of the young abductees who were kept as sex slaves had died under physical torture. Some Indian former cooks and gardeners who worked for a rich Sheikh claimed to have identified two boys working in a house for a person closely related to the Al Maktoum family. "The burly Sheikh," said Suresh Wadekar, a former cook, originally from Mumbai, India, "is now spending his last days in a posh hospital. Both the boys were brought here from Turkey. We thought they were Turkish children!"

Reports state that the Sheikh had them physically restrained by chains to their ankles and tied to the bed. They were unchained when the cruel Sheikh molested them and had his guests also do the same. We do not know his real name until this day. Another Indian national stated that upon employment and arrival at the Sheikh's residence, they were ordered to address him as "Master," with heads bowed and added that he saw dozens of portraits of the Al Maktoum family members in his vast living room with himself besides them in every picture. The bodies of the dead youths were simply hauled by a furniture moving truck, their destiny unknown.

Of late, reports claimed that dozens of young Jewish women from Moldova have entered Turkey on their way to immigrate to Israel without informing the Jewish Agencies of their intentions to migrate to Israel. "They voluntarily decide to go to Israel via Turkey and that is their greatest mistake," said a reporter writing for the London Times. On arrival, trafficking agents meet these women promising them a three or six months work with substantial pay so that they could have enough money on their arrival in Israel. It is then that their misery begins. Within hours, a few of the better-looking ones are put on a van and spirited off to Istanbul to commence a life of sex-slaves for visiting rich tourists. Their destinies are often unknown since they are not registered or expected by anyone in Israel.

Similarly, Jewish women from Ukraine, who stop in Turkey for some easy money to proceed later to Israel, face the same fate. In Kiev, newspapers regularly warn young girls to refrain from believing promises of thousands of dollars a month in Istanbul and to report agents who approach them.

The Kiev police have so far arrested a dozen or more agents; most of them Russians who have direct connection with customers in Istanbul. The customers in Istanbul are in reality brothel owners who cater to the need of Arab businesspersons from the Persian Gulf Sheikhdoms who leave their residences and family behind on the pretext of signing important business deals.

Of subtle interest is the fact that the overall ownership of brothels in Istanbul belongs to Arabs, mostly from Bahrain, Saudi Arabia Dubai, Qatar, and Sharjah, a part of the United Arab Emirates. The majority of their customers are in turn from Dubai, Saudi Arabia and Kuwait.

A spokesperson for the "Women Enslavement" affiliated to the Police in Istanbul in the first week of May 2012 said that authorities arrested a certain Saudi National said to be the coordinator of importing sex slaves from Russia, Ukraine, Belarus, Moldova, Romania and Bulgaria. His name was not divulged due to unknown reasons. It was learned that he was freed within a few minutes as soon as he was taken to the police precinct.

The head of the "Women Enslavement" task force of the Istanbul police said that repeated calls to all the women abducted or those enslaved to find ways and means to contact them or any law enforcement authorities have been futile. The women-slaves have no access to a phone or any means to communicate. The officer said that as soon as the customers of a certain slave diminish, she is quietly driven to a far off destination, but preferably inside nearby Bulgaria. An added cruelty is that their documents are never returned to them causing them further hardships and forcing them into a life of uncertainty and further misery.

Writer Craig S. Smith of the New York Times reported in June 28, 2005 that: "Most come of their own free will to Turkey, but many end up as virtual slaves, sold from pimp to pimp through a loosely organized slave and criminal network that stretches from Moscow to Istanbul and beyond."

It is a common sight in the streets of Chisinau (Moldova), Sofia (Bulgaria), Bucharest (Romania) and smaller cities and villages in the Balkans to come across agents who will pay a few Euros to informers of the existence and whereabouts of young girls and boys whose family are desperately poor and in need of some money. As usual, most of the victims end up in Saudi Arabia, Kuwait and the entire Sheikhdoms of the United Arab Emirates to serve as slaves to the rich.

Unlike the Arab countries and others like China and Iran, the succeeding Turkish governments have never been involved in either the encouragement or the toleration of slave labor; this is at least since the past seventy years. Turkey, like most of the Arab countries is a strong ally of the USA and has very close ties to Israel. Turkey receives billions of dollars in aid, most of it in weapons.

Nepal

> "All pain is either severe or slight, if slight, it is easily endured; if severe, it will without doubt be brief."
>
> Marcus Tullius Cicero

The late King Birendra of Nepal (1945-2001) in mid 1999 was asked to elaborate the problems his Kingdom faced. He responded by saying, "Young children being abducted from the various parts of my country and taken over to India by numerous human traffickers and ultimately led to a life of slavery in India where their lives are condemned to be brief and cruel."

This has been going on since the past century, even during the time of British rule in the Indian Subcontinent. More than ten thousand are simply abducted or just dragged from their homes for a few Indian Rupees paid to their unsuspecting parents. The parents are convinced that their daughters will have a very good life in India ultimately going to some University over there!

When asked of his plans to remedy this ill by a Human Rights reporter, after some thoughts, the King vowed that beginning the year 2000; he will personally lead a crusade, to destroy the roots of this evil. "I will employ the services of former members of the elite 'Gurkha Brigade' from Britain and India since I am aware that nearly 50 percent of them return to their ancestral land in Nepal after leaving their services. I will be merciless to these agents and brokers in human body!"

The crusade was still in planning stage when the King and his entire family were massacred on June 1, 2001 at a royal dinner party. Dipendra, the eldest son of the King shot most of the members of the Royal family and he too died later of a self-inflicted gunshot wound. Thus came to an end any hope of even mounting the crusade on the evils of trafficking in Nepal. Human trafficking continues unabated.

U.S. State Department Trafficking in Persons Report, June 2009 states: "Nepal is a source country for men; women and children trafficked for the purposes of commercial sexual exploitation and involuntary servitude. Children are trafficked within the country and to India and the Middle East for commercial sexual exploitation."

NGOs estimate that 10,000 to 15,000 Nepali women and girls are trafficked annually to India, while 7,500 children are trafficked domestically for commercial sexual exploitation. The young boys as young as eight and nine are sexually exploited and then sold to Arabs in the Persian Gulf Sheikhdoms. Almost not a single "boy-slave" has grown into adulthood and there are no reports of any returning back to Nepal.

The number of young girls and women trafficked to India does not include the nearly similar and alarming figure of underage girls, boys and adult women taken over the border into India for the sole purpose of being exported to other countries, mainly to Arab countries. After all, they are commodities in the eyes of agents and brokers. It is most shocking that these human beings are placed in various batches for various countries. The Saudi customers often appreciate boys as well as girls, whereas the Sheikhdoms in the Emirates only buy girls. The majority of sex-slaves for Bahrain are boys.

"I witnessed helplessly when they were being separated and segregated; these girls for this Sheikhdom and those girls for that Sheikhdom and Kingdom! Only tags and labels were not put on these human beings destined for a miserable life," said Arjun Thapa, a former member of the elite Gurkha Brigade in India.

Surya B. Prasai writing in "The American Chronicle" on February 10, 2008 described the alarming fact of the unique cultural system known as "Deukis" in Nepal. A rich individual having no children through a legally married wife, procure these young girls, often between ten and fifteen years of age from poor Nepalese rural families for adoption.

Inquiries reveal that later after initiating, the young girls through Hindu rituals in a temple, become mistresses and slave bonded laborers to produce offspring. As the girl gets to be over thirty years or grows older and unappealing, she is discarded and forced into prostitution. There is no description to the sufferings of the Nepalese girl once initiated into this age-old system.

According to statistics obtained from various Welfare Organizations in Nepal, the number of Deukis by May 2012 had risen to an astonishing figure of fifty thousand! This figure is greatly increased when compared to the United Nations reports that there were over thirty thousand girls identified as "Deukis" in 2007. The same agency reported that they numbered around seventeen thousand in 1997.

Several independent investigations revealed that the other ills of abduction, trafficking, buying, and selling human beings in Nepal also related to the ultimate crime against humanity. They all end in various forms of slavery; chief among them being forced labor and sex-slaves. Premature death is the result of these two deeds.

Democratic People's Republic of Korea (North Korea)

> "Lawless are they that make their wills their laws!"
>
> Shakespeare

A country and its administrative elites doing whatever they please to nearly twenty five million people whose lives they have wrapped in a cocoon of mystery and closed to any foreign reporter.

It is increasingly a challenge to investigate and research the condition of the general population under a secretive regime since 1945 when Kim Il-sung seized power. To this day, it is felt better to strike verbally at that regime for its gross enslavement of its people than to hypothetically prepare statements.

On May 28, 2012, popular journalist of the CNN television channel Paula Hancocks exposed the once only thought about notoriety of the regime. "Watching the public execution of his mother and older brother, Shin Dong-hyuk thought the punishment was just. They had planned to escape the North Korean labor camp they were being held in until Shin overheard them and reported them to the prison guards."

Young Shin was brainwashed to accept the ideologies of the State and to go to the extent of condemning his own parents! He felt no remorse for being instrumental in the execution of his mother and brother. The notorious ideologies taught children to spy on their parents.

North Korea has become the most notorious country in the world for depriving its people of their basic rights. It has tormented, tortured and even murdered them in cold blood for the least infraction of the so-called Laws of the State.

Kim Jung-un, the baby-faced despot who took up the mantle of his father and grandfather has shown to be merciless and as despotic as his father and grandfather. On the December 12, 2013, the new dictator arrested and put to death his uncle, Jang-Song-thaek, in the cruelest manner ever conceivable. Reports claim that aides brought in more than a hundred dogs to feed on his corpse. The charges were that he was contemplating a military coup.

Independent reports also claimed that more than fifty near and distant relatives of Jang were put to death by the orders of Kim Jung-un. Some were diplomats while a few dozen were military officials of the regime.

In early March 2014, reports from Pyongyang gave the most horrific report. Loyal guards to the young despot buried hundreds of men, women, and children in ditches on suspicion of indifference to his lectures. All were still alive when a bulldozer covered them. Days later, after this news, a former bodyguard of Kim Jong-un, who had escaped to the South, verified the news.

Hundreds of labor camps exist throughout the country. Entire family members receive harsh punishments, ranging from imprisonment to torture and executions for the crimes of a single person. This is very similar to the one practiced in the Islamic Theocracy in Iran.

Dozens of prison camps sprung up in the early 1950's to mercilessly crush dissent. Documents proved that tens of thousands of opponents were simply shot or buried alive under the regime of Kim Il-sung who was the acclaimed hero of North Korea and given the title of the "Eternal President of the Republic."

Of encouragement to the outside world is that South Korea's government is attempting to document the atrocities for the first time, collecting disturbing firsthand accounts from those who have managed to make it to South Korea, including the elder Shin who escaped in 2004. A 381-page report from the National Human Rights Commission of Korea is based on the testimony of 278 defectors has recently been published with names of prison guards who carried out torture or executions.

The Kim dynasty has mercilessly strangled the general population through imprisonment, starvation and forced labor. There is no pardon from this newly appointed leader. Kim Jong-un took over from his late father in December 2011 while the world hoped for a change in the brutal laws of the State. North Korea under him became a massive prison with him as the jailer. All members of the Kim dynasty were and are repressive, cruel and murderous. Repressions and open crime against its population is not new to the rulers of North Korea. Murder, enslavement, torture, rape and forced abortions are common in the land where a family has been ruling since 1945.

Kingdom of Thailand

"Death is better than slavery"

Harriett Ann Jacobs

Statements from "Human Trafficking and Modern Day Slavery" describe Thailand as a source, transit and destination country for men, women and children trafficked for the purposes of forced labor and commercial sexual exploitation.

Thailand's relative prosperity attracts migrants from neighboring countries and from as far away from Russia and Fiji who flee conditions of poverty, and in the case of Myanmar (Burma), military repression. Significant illegal migration to Thailand presents traffickers with opportunities to force, coerce, or defraud undocumented migrants into involuntary servitude or sexual exploitation.

Men, women and children are trafficked from Myanmar into Thailand for forced-labor in fishing-related industries, factories, agriculture, construction, domestic work and begging. Women and children are also trafficked from Myanmar, Cambodia, Laos, Vietnam, Russia, Uzbekistan and the People's Republic of China for commercial sexual-exploitation in Thailand.

In an article, dated May 14, 2007, in the Thai paper, "Nation" adapted from "The misery of male slavery," quoting the "Human Trafficking Organization," prominent Thai writer Subhatra Bhumprabhas points to disturbing developments in Thailand. "The fight against human trafficking has for more than a decade tried to protect women and children, often forgetting that men, too, are victims of 'new slavery' and that constitute men in very large numbers."

The Human Trafficking Organization also notes that between July 17 and July 19, 2003, six fishing trawlers with a crew of about a hundred sailed from Tha Chalom in Samut Sakhon province to fish in Indonesian territorial waters. Most of the crewmembers were migrant workers and four were younger than sixteen. The Organization added that, "Of the hundred crew members thirty eight did not return, dying on the job. Two were buried in one of the several islands of Indonesia while the rest were dumped into the sea. One died immediately on his return to Thailand while the rest were seriously ill."

Speaking on the condition of anonymity, a former member of the Thai Parliament in mid 2006 said; "We have hundreds and hundreds of kilometers of coastline where we have thousands of small and large units of fish-farms who use sea water for clams, shrimps of various sizes and even fish employing slave labor."

In mid 2007, there was a report damning the Labor Ministry from a group of Thai people who carefully investigated the deplorable situation of laborers on these fish farms. The majority of them turned out to be slave-laborers. Those whose origin was Thai were from the several hill tribes in the north of the country. Shocking but true, these people although from Thailand have no legal status in the country! The rest were from Cambodia, Laos, and Myanmar. None of them spoke Thai properly. They just understood orders. Dried fish with the cheapest quality of rice was their only source of food.

At least fifty countries in the world import fish and shrimps including crustaceans from Thailand. None has taken any step to investigate the source of labor producing their imports. Slavery thrives in various forms in this country where Buddhism, the religion of peace is the national religion.

Records show that a minimum of four thousand slave-laborers die each year in various parts of the country as a result of mistreatment, malnutrition and beatings. The belongings of the dead victims do not go beyond a pair of worn out sandals and a pair of extra short pant and shirt.

The Bangkok Post on July 18, 2007 urged more action against slave labor. It was a self-serving article, which did not suggest any form of remedy or steps to ameliorate this evil.

There is no proper channel in Thailand to lodge any complaint against slave labor. No government official ever agrees to reflect this misery in the Parliament or on air. The King and Queen of that country are simply out of bounds to the general public or even foreign reporters and worshipped by the same people who have no right to either see them or receive any form of reply to their grievances.

Young girls and boys being forced into a life of slavery is common in Thailand and very little if anything at all is being done to put an end to this crime. Stray cases however manage to surface where kidnappers transported a young Thai woman in a plane bound for Bangkok's Suvarnabhumi airport. Human Right's activists identified the sickly and frail woman as a slave-woman returned either from Saudi Arabia or any of the Sheikhdoms of the United Arab Emirates or Kuwait. Her sorrow does not end on arrival to her native land. She dies a week later. Airport officials claim that at least three women return daily from the Persian Gulf region. At least 20 percent previously held in bondage would die within the next two years while another fifty percent will succumb to their illness in a period of five years. The causes are mostly untreated illness or the result of continuous rapes and beatings.

A report by Pattaya Daily News in early 2012 claimed that the average age of the women returning was thirty. They are identified as those fortunate to survive the ordeal of slavery in life; at least for the time being. They were smuggled out of Thailand at an average age of twelve to any of the several Arab countries located in the Persian Gulf.

The Daily, elsewhere in the past had drawn the attention of the world to a series of examples where young Thai girls whose last address was in Saudi Arabia, Bahrain, Kuwait and the Emirates had not answered any more telephone calls or letters by their parents. They had either perished one way or the other, death by illness or simply murdered. Thousands die each year as slaves to the Arabs in the Persian Gulf countries and hundreds commit suicide and thousands more are kidnapped by traffickers while fleeing their Arab masters and forced into another life of slavery in other less known and smaller Sheikhdoms. The young girls abducted from Thailand are sold to an agent who in turn sells them to a customer.

Another shameful aspect of slavery is that along the Thai-Myanmar borders there are brokers who invest in young women to sell them later. The "Nation" newspaper on February 3, 2007 reported that twenty long-necked Karen women (Paduang) were arrested and later freed while crossing the Thai-Myanmar border, accompanied by agents who had tricked them by offering them high salaried jobs in Hotels in Bangkok. These agents are often referred to as "Phuket investors."

The Asahi Shimbun reported on June 9, 2006 from Tokyo that rings of human smugglers have been unearthed operating between Thailand and Japan. Further investigations proved that during the last five decades, very young girls were smuggled into Japan, mostly by sea in trawlers. The human cargo was unloaded at various areas of the coastline and sent to the various destinations in several parts of the Island Nation. Groups of young girls purchased in a one-time deal through agents from Thailand and delivered to Japanese clients. They were termed as "delivery parcels."

Unconfirmed news, rampant in many business circles in Japan claim many senior officials of major Japanese companies have small apartments scattered throughout Tokyo, Osaka, Nagoya and elsewhere where very young girls are kept as virtual slaves. Reports claim they are rarely allowed to venture out except under the watchful eyes of a bulky maidservant accompanying them. In one article, the Shimbun in the early days of January 2012 made a faint reference about the unknown whereabouts of "grown-up" slave girls of the past, and found no trace of them either leaving Japan or even dying. Such unfortunates are also called the "disposable human beings" born to simply serve the conscienceless rich in Japan.

Independent investigators, mostly government officials of Japan interested to unearth the slave-trade which is almost promoted by owners of production units or company Presidents, claim that at any given time there are between twenty five thousand and forty thousand young slave-girls scattered all over Japan. They are Thai, Burmese, Cambodian, Laotian, Vietnamese, Korean and even Chinese girls to serve the wealthy strata as slaves without any payment, slaves with no form of basic rights whatsoever and at the total mercy of the Japanese rich. The bulk of the girls are kidnapped or snatched from their parents in daylight from nearly all the regions of Thailand. Some were bought.

In Japan, there is no news on the television or radio about these atrocities against humanity; there are no discussions on any platform to voice such matters. Senior Government officials claim it is blasphemy against the country and to discuss such matters would be also against the Emperor, and anything against the Emperor is sedition and treason against the Japanese Nation! Such an act has no relations whatsoever to the Japanese Emperor.

EUROPE

"Those who will not reason are bigots, those who cannot, are
fools, and those who dare not, are slaves."

George Gordon Byron

There is a great degree of resemblance of the movements, forced migrations, origins and destinations of girls destined to become sex-slaves to the most odious form of slavery. In the Asian Continent, girls from various Asian countries are trafficked to other Asian countries and a smaller percentage to other Continents. Likewise, teenage girls from various parts of Europe are sent to other countries in Europe, while a small number end up in other Continents. The movements and migrations appear to be in a circle, as if catering to the needs of clients globally.

Federal Republic of Germany

"The fundamental sense of freedom is freedom from chains,
from imprisonment, from enslavement by others. The rest is
extension of this sense, or else metaphor."

Isaiah Berlin

Investigations and official reports by both several non-governmental organizations, the International Labor Organization and the various agencies of the United Nations dealing with Human Rights have pointed towards the Federal Republic of Germany as the hub of slavery for Europe. More precisely forced prostitution of kidnapped and trafficked women, some as young as twelve with doctored papers. Most of them are from neighboring European countries, particularly from the Balkans.

The Federal German Government has repeatedly rejected any accusation that it is either condoning or allowing slavery to be practiced. At no given time, has the Federal German Government ever alluded to the tens of thousands of kidnapped underage girls forced into a life of prostitution to earn money for their owners, groups or individuals who bought these girls from traffickers.

In late 2011, Angela Merkel the Chancellor of the Federal Republic of Germany was asked by a reporter of "Free Press International" a brief question while having alighted from her heavily guarded vehicle, if there were any problems with slavery or child prostitution in Germany to which she responded: "We have no slave ever worthy of being mentioned. There is no slave or slavery of any kind in our country now or in the past!"

Based on Ms. Merkel's claims, one invokes the statements of Victor Hugo in Les Miserables. "We say that slavery has vanished from European civilization, but this is not true. Slavery still exists, but now it applies only to women and its name is prostitution."

One may shudder and even feel chagrined at learning that the Federal Republic of Germany is a magnet; the focal point of slave trade in females, anywhere from the age of twelve to fifty. The younger ones, below nineteen, defined as underage by law, have doctored documents to protect their owners from legal pursuit if arrested.

At any given time, trafficked victims turned into sex-slaves throughout the country number more than fifty thousand with nearly 80 percent of them being from European countries. From the Baltic States to the Balkans, from different places in the African Continent to south East Asia, girls, young women, and even young boys are smuggled to Germany to serve the needs of the corrupt and vile.

The very dependable statistics presented by the U.S. Department of State Bureau of Democracy, Human Rights and Labor dated March 8, 2006 gave a chilling report on the status and conditions facing the sex-slave victims in the Federal Republic of Germany. In 2003 alone, more than a thousand two hundred slave-girls managed to escape from the homes and apartments of their owners and address themselves to the nearest police precinct.

"Traffickers used a range of intimidation techniques to ensure the compliance of victims, including threats of deportation, misrepresentation of victims' legal rights and status, physical violence, and withholding travel and identification documents," the U.S. report stated.

The same report in 2006 also stated that the number of sex-slaves who managed to escape and introduce themselves to the law had multiplied four times, virtually four thousand five hundred. In 2007, a staggering figure of more than twelve thousand sex-slaves had managed to free themselves from human bondage and slavery, thanks to several Catholic Nuns who secretly worked away from their "Order" and their duties, delivered freedom to the enslaved girls through the law. The whole episode was kept a tight secret so as not to embarrass the political elites of the German government.

These sex-slaves were in Hamburg, Frankfurt, Munich, Dusseldorf, Cologne, Stuttgart, Bonn, Berlin and a few far-flung villages in the south of the country. One of the Nuns requesting anonymity said, "We had help; assistance from several dedicated people, ex-police officials, retired army officers, postal employees and even a sizeable number of Bank employees. All coordinated and cooperated closely for nearly one year to bring about the collapse of this ring of horror, but this situation returns, which means the mission must continue."

Many victims were enslaved in the most atrocious medieval methods. They were chained with lightweight aluminum chains while some were tied up with ropes in large walk-in-closets and a few good number were tied to their beds in a room filled with torture implements.

The rescue of thousands of slave-girls did not spell the end of this cruelty. In fact, in mid February 2011, "Radio Free Europe" stated that the Italian police had arrested forty-one Bulgarians who had been trafficking hundreds of young girls with falsified documents for enslavement purpose to German citizens. Another seventy five agents were arrested in Austria and Italy in the same year and were ultimately found to have trafficked more than two thousand young girls from Albania, Croatia, Macedonia, Serbia and Montenegro in a span of two years; 2007-2009. All were destined to Germany. It was also discovered upon interrogation of the arrested agents, that a few had lost their lives due to illness and fatigue. Most of them were buried in the woods. All the buyers from the German side were people of German origin. Among them were several women.

What is most alarming is that the modus operandi in trafficking is virtually the same throughout the world. The only difference is that some of the victims are transported by air while many on boats and a good number through land routes. Whether in Thailand or in India or in the Balkans, or even in Central Europe, these unfortunate females are bought and sold as if they were produce, utensils, or garments. Both the buyer and the seller consider them as disposable beings.

Hannah Cleaver writing for "The Telegraph" on March 1, 2003 in an article titled: "Woman Judge that ran sex ring that killed boy aged five," described a gory picture of a former woman judge who had once sworn to uphold the law. The judge identified as Christa W. owns a brothel disguised as a pub in Berlin.

Cleaver reported that the abuse took place in the back room of a pub run by the former judge. The bar was a meeting place for drug dealers and prostitutes. Several other news reports suggest that she took money from customers for access to the children.

Police reports stated that a boy of five identified as Pascal was beaten by one of her customers while being abused to keep him quiet and that the boy died due to a blow to his skull. The abusers then drove the dead boy to the border where they buried him in the presence of the former judge.

In comparison to the slave-owners in Arab countries, the majority of the owners in Germany are comparatively benign and magnanimous where the unfortunates are concerned. The victim is usually released with a small amount, enough for her travel expenses back home, but the unfortunate one is too deep in misery to return. She goes on to other countries with lower economies and thereby turns herself into a willing-slave with lesser expectations. The often foul-mouthed and burly German owner wittingly and unwittingly paves the way for the further creation of unfortunate women by turning his craves for younger slave girls who are always in abundance.

In Stuttgart, a social and welfare worker from the Salvation Army noted that she investigated the background of more than a dozen slave owners. At least 90 percent of them were married and owned thriving businesses or were executive officers of large corporations and banks. Of subtle interest, she noted, that all owned small studios where they housed their unfortunate victims. With no travel documents or any form of identity papers, the unfortunate ones were condemned to a life of slavery until they were disposed of and replaced by newer and younger girls.

Angela Merkel, the Chancellor of Germany has shown very little interest, if not, absolute reluctance to discuss this misery at a national level. Similarly, so far, there has not been the faintest voice from any member of the Bundestag mentioning any suggestion to even include this subject in any of their agendas to address the situation plaguing the German nation and society.

In June 7, 2006, the Deutsche Welle reported that in Berlin, an unidentified woman unsuccessfully attempted to approach Angela Merkel, the German Chancellor, to present her with a petition reflecting the onerous situation of women slaves in the country and the horrifying condition of men employed by private coalmine owners. Most of the developments took place in the lower Lusatia and in the North Rhine-Westphalia regions.

Most of the men who lived and worked in slave-like conditions in mines and farms were undocumented workers from Poland, Greece, Romania, Moldova, Bulgaria, the Czech Republic, Slovakia and Turkey. They were forced to work for twelve hours, with a thirty-minute break for lunch, which was a simple sandwich. They were paid a one-euro coin for every day they worked! They were housed in trailer houses where nearly twenty people were crammed in unhygienic conditions. It is unknown how many have succumbed to illnesses due to the conditions in the mines, or the poor living conditions, or a host of other reasons. No details were available and no foreign mass media ever reported this incident.

Now is the time for a direct intervention by the German Federal Government to recognize and coordinate with several societies and non-governmental organizations within Germany and throughout the world in order to bring about a better living condition for thousands of people living and working in slave-like conditions. Now is the time to actively air the grievances for the tens of thousands of voiceless young girls held in chains and fetters. Now is the right time to embark on a mission to liberate those unfortunate men and women laboring in coal and other mines until their last breath on earth. Now is the time!

Without such a daring and historical move, not much could be expected to ameliorate their lives in a country notorious for infringement of Human Rights but rarely mentioned or ever condemned in any Resolution by any International Organization.

Russian Federation (Russia)

> "Those who deny freedom to others deserve it not for themselves."
>
> Abraham Lincoln

Reports from Human Trafficking and Modern-Day Slavery list Russia as a source, transit and destination country for men, women and children trafficked for the purposes of forced labor and commercial sexual exploitation. Slavery in all its manifestation is the direct result of such acts.

Russia with an area exceeding seventeen million square kilometers (6,592,800 square miles) is the largest country in the world with a population of 143 million people, also has a high percentage of existing slavery; millions enchained within the country while nearly two hundred thousand Russians enslaved abroad, with no future and no hope.

On March 5, 2004, Anatoly Medetsky writing in the Moscow Times mentioned that there were at the present four million slaves of various denominations and descriptions in the Federation of Russia. "The figures ever increase; they are increasing at an alarming rate, so frightening that by the end of 2010 it is predicted the figure will augment to nearly five million, if not more." The Report was titled "Forced Labor in Contemporary Russia."

Since the past two decades, various forms of social ills and exigencies have been afflicting the successive Russian governments with a direct effect on the general Russian society. The Non-Communist governments have conspicuously failed to deliver prosperity unto any sector where the common Russian is related. The blame falls on the shoulders of the Soviet Union, which failed its citizens and failed to deliver what the ideals of International Communism and Marxism had promised. A quick glimpse on the records of Marxist regimes in any country narrates a history in grief, poverty, enslavement, hunger and a host of miseries.

Ills and miseries in the past have always been blamed on the Soviet philosophy of life and the prescriptions of Marxism which have proved to be a failure and which still has its effect on the general population. Every economic failure, which had relations to social problems, was then attributed to the infamy of the Bolshevik Revolution and at the present to the self-serving politicians. After the collapse of the Soviet Union, a myriad of blames have been focused on the ruling elite as those being directly responsible for the continuing calamity that has befallen the Russian family.

Gorbachev and his group were ousted, so was the Soviet Union and so was the Marxist-Leninist ideology to be replaced by a murky Russian approach to life and living. It was not successful. It failed. Mother Russia was sinking and sinking fast. Within five years of the end of Communist rule, the much-expected paradise of Capitalism did not arrive as expected. The masses did not benefit from it then and now. The unscrupulous few, numbering some fifty thousand out of a population of nearly 143 million people have managed to become millionaires and even billionaires within ten years.

This is unbelievable yet true. Most of these millionaires and billionaires have servants living in absolute servitude to them. The majority of these laborers who have no belonging in the least or any money in their pockets are usually from the far-flung regions of Russia. Prominent among those trafficked for slave labor is the Tatar, Bashkir, Chechens and the Chuvash.

The International Labor Organization in a report dated June 2009 stated that labor trafficking is the most predominant form of trafficking in Russia. Slave labor forms the core of the private economy. Men, women and children are trafficked from Ukraine, Moldova, Kyrgyzstan,

Tajikistan, and Uzbekistan into Russia and then sold into slavery with every individual having different purposes of service to the owners. Minorities from other parts of Russia form the bulk of slave labor of the rich. Most of the owners are members of the former Communist Party of the Soviet Union.

Similarly, men, women and children from the Russian Far East are trafficked to South Korea, China, Bahrain, Oman, Japan and Dubai for the purposes of sex slavery, debt bondage and slave labor. The men are forced to work in agricultural and fishing sectors while the women are held in captivity as the private property of the owner. The U.S. State Department Trafficking in Person Report on June 2009 stated that some Russian women are trafficked to Turkey, Greece, South Africa, Israel, Poland, Italy, Spain, Vietnam, Thailand, New Zealand, Saudi Arabia, and Australia for the purpose of commercial sexual exploitation. A large number of them however, end up becoming slaves.

A shocking news by Radio Free Europe on October 21, 2004 voiced concern about the lives of more than thirty thousand Russian children who are reported missing every year with nearly half a million young children in the streets who live in appalling conditions. The more than thirty thousand children, who are listed as missing, are in fact those abducted and sold into slavery never to be seen again. Private printing companies throughout the country specialize in the preparation of falsified birth certificates for the victims to be trafficked to countries from where demands for young girls are in abundance.

Leonid Chekalin, who heads the organization "Children are Russia's Future," in February 2011 said nearly five hundred trafficking networks dealing with the kidnapping of underage children have been uncovered during the past five years and many more remained to be discovered.

Pravda, still a major newspaper, in early 2011 reported that, investigation results by four independent organizations and societies in the Russian Federation showed that more than a thousand trafficking networks exist throughout the country. The majority of the victims are mostly young underage girls and to a lesser extent young boys and teenagers. The larger percentage of the networks caters to people in Germany, Japan, Saudi Arabia, the United Arab Emirates and China. The report suggested that as much as a hundred thousand victims are trafficked each year to European countries while a similar figure to elsewhere in the world.

Russian human smugglers coordinate their activities with the "Merchants of Misery;" Russian brokers in slavery, in supplying young Russian girls to wherever required. The smugglers are the ones who scout regions in various parts of the world and fulfill the orders with themselves being the partner in crime.

Radio Free Europe in late 2011 broadcasted appeals to the parents all over the Russian Federation and the Confederation of Independent States, asking them to prevent their children from meeting dubious people through the internet and predicted a life of perpetual slavery if they ever consent to travel abroad under false promises.

Beginning January 2000 until early 2012, Anti-Slavery International has published thousands of Case Studies stating construction workers were being trafficked from Russia to South West Europe on false promises of jobs and good payments. More than ten thousand cases were cited by various Societies for the prevention of slave labor in Europe. These figures are the ones unearthed. Those luckless often die on the construction site where they work and are immediately disposed of in methods yet unknown. They do not even form any statistic. They are not considered as having died. Their deaths are not recorded.

The unfortunate ones who are gullible are smuggled usually into Spain, Portugal and Germany where they labor in construction sites surrounded by barbed wire without pay for several months. Their passports and identity papers are taken from them for "safekeeping" but very seldom returned to them. They become slaves as soon as they land in the country of destination. A good percent of them manage to escape after months but physical debilitation and illness caused by exhaustion overwhelms many of them who simply die in the streets.

Agence France-Presse on February 12, 2005 reported the gravity of enslavement in Russia, which it called beyond horror. Russia's Far East newspapers advertise promising and well-paying jobs, usually a receptionist, salesperson, cashier, a family governess, and other such alluring offers, which are in reality a trap, a dangerous trap that spells the end of life for a person if victimized. In the eastern port city of Vladivostok, the weekly "Dalpress" publishes ten to twenty such ads in each issue. Other newspapers and magazines in the same region print hundreds of announcements for employment opportunities in Japan, Macao and Israel.

On March 31, 2005, Pravda wrote an article warning young girls not to be lured into traps of misery and enslavement by unscrupulous announcements of a better life and wealth in Israel. The article said: "It is difficult for the girls to escape when in Israel; many appeal to the Russian Embassy for help. Correspondents of the 'Novye Izvestia' newspaper learnt in Tel Aviv, people connected with recruiters of sex slaves stand close to the Embassy and do not let them escape."

Human Rights Reports in early 2006 stated that Russian women have been trafficked to almost fifty countries, including the majority of West European countries, U.S.A., Canada, Middle East and several other Asian countries. Traffickers usually target young girls, some as young as fourteen but not exceeding twenty-five. The reports indicated that internal trafficking fueled by poverty and unemployment was the main cause. Almost all those trafficked, whether the victims of internal trafficking or otherwise became slaves at the time of their transfer.

Immediately after the fall of the Soviet Union, the larger areas of the country's borders were virtually open. Hundreds of checkpoints were dismantled due to financial exigencies and this helped traffickers who were already operating, albeit in very negligible number to multiply within days. Trafficking human beings for the purpose of slave labor and sex slave abroad became a business and a profession in the Russian Federation. More than fifty thousand people are now employed in this diabolical trade.

Vladimir Radyuhin in an article in the "Hindu" dated May 30, 2004 presented the reasons for the sudden increase in the trade of human beings from the Russian Federation. "After the break-up of the Soviet Union in 1991, Russia emerged a major channel of human smuggling from Asia to the West. Global networks used Russia's porous borders, legal loopholes and corruption to haul illegal migrants, from Asia to Europe."

Repeatedly it has been reported by various Human Rights Organizations that Russian consulates in Asian countries would rubberstamp hundreds of tourist visas based on fraudulent invitations sent in by non-existent Russian firms, while Russian border guards would look the other way when crowds of so-called tourists crossed the border into Russian territory.

Earlier, in June 2002, Prof. Donna M. Hughes prepared a report for the International Organization for Migration in which she reflected a multitude of reasons why the trafficking business thrives in Russia. Apart from the porous borders, which are a help, great profits can be made by the traffickers, corruption of officials and police at many levels and reluctance of lawmakers to intervene due in part of reprisals by violent criminal syndicates.

On June 18, 2003, Prof. Hughes claimed that the Russian Federation has received failing grades from the U.S. State Department for its efforts to combat trafficking leading to slavery. Research indicated each year; thousands of women and girls are trafficked for prostitution, sex slavery or directly sold into slavery. The total number over the past decade is estimated to be over half a million. Organized-crime groups run the trafficking networks that have sold Russian girls into prostitution and sex slavery in over fifty countries around the world, including the United States.

Newspapers in Europe regularly report the arrest of traffickers and their superiors in nearly all the Scandinavian countries and the Benelux where they openly set up business and even advertise their possibilities in supplying young women as escorts. This is a concealed and coded definition for young and often underage girls with doctored papers from Russia.

The buyer often knows the true purpose of the newspaper advertisements, a slave girl for a few thousand Euros! Once bought, the owner forces the girl into prostitution. Often the owner has several prostitutes working for him. On attaining a certain age, they are thrown out where the victims have few destinations in life left to them. Many end up in brothels where they contract severe illnesses, commit suicide or are just killed by dangerous elements in the streets.

The abominable situation of slavery in the Russian Federation cannot be measured or described in a few volumes, let alone a chapter. The damage done unto the people through traffickers in the past two decades has taken its toll: two million and more human beings in slavery. A similar figure in forced labor while ten times that figure in abject poverty and rising unabatedly. These are the horrors inside the Russian Federation whose leaders reflect irrelevance to any internal problem, particularly related to human rights.

After the fall of Communism, Presidents Boris Yeltsin, Vladimir Putin and Dmitry Medvedev continued to call for a change in the labor laws of the country and even went to the extent of asking the public to change their very lifestyle in order to bring about a radical change for the betterment of the society in general. They also insisted in their monologues that remembering the past was only a waste of time.

Research has shown that no labor reform has been initiated in Russia since the last two decades. There was no mention by any members of the Duma (Russian parliament) about the appalling condition of workers held in bondage and those laboring as bonded slaves.

All said, there are no correct or even approximate figures for those held in slavery in Russia although it is in millions.

> "Everyone thinks of changing the world, but no one thinks of changing himself."
>
> Lev Nikolayevich Tolstoy

Ireland

> "When we abolish the slavery of half of humanity, together
> with the whole system of hypocrisy, it implies, the 'division' of
> humanity will reveal its genuine significance and the human
> couple will find its true form."
>
> Simone de Beauvoir

Slavery in the yesteryears and today

In late 2006 Patrick Ahern, the then Taoiseach (head of the government or Prime Minister of Ireland) was approached by a women's group demanding to know if any steps have been taken to combat slavery of very young children in Ireland. Next, he was asked as to what he knew about the unabated smuggling of underage children from Bulgaria, Poland, Czech Republic, Slovakia and several countries from Africa into Ireland and then sold to dealers in France, England and Germany. The seemingly annoyed Prime Minister responded: "We never had and we do not have slaves in Ireland. There were no Irish slaves anywhere so we have no individuals enslaved in Ireland either. Ireland is not the trafficking route either."

But Ireland also had Eamon de Valera, President of the Executive council of Ireland between 1932-1937 who had boldly suggested that if there were any remaining vestiges of human trafficking or slavery left in Ireland he would be the person to confront it without any fear from either the traffickers or those politicians who were either indifferent to this act of evil or who in private supported the criminals in doing it. De Valera had some significant success then until the advent of the Second World War. After the end of the war, he picked up his fight against traffickers until the end of his life. He had proposed the maximum sentence, although he did not specify it, for the traffickers and the agents including those behind this business.

In 2007, major newspapers in Ireland had hopes that a new incoming government would actively involve itself in curbing the slave trade in Ireland that was virtually exploding. Ireland had become a route for traffickers from Europe, Asia and Africa.

Independent Irish Senator Ronan Mullen took the bold initiative to call for serious steps to be taken to deal with the prevailing slave trade and to prevent Ireland from being a route for slaves to be transported elsewhere once they are smuggled into Ireland. "The incoming government must act quickly to criminalize human trafficking and to protect the victims of this trade," Senator Mullen told the "Independent."

On February 14, 2011, the "Trafficking in Persons Report" by the US State Department reveals that during 2006 and onwards, Zambian girls were trafficked to Ireland and the United Kingdom "for the purpose of forced labor."

The "Wexford Echo" reported on August 13, 2007 that a major new study has commissioned to determine the scale of illegal trafficking into Ireland. The research was commissioned in the wake of the shocking revelation that children are routinely smuggled through Rosslare Harbor. A few days later on September 4, 2007, the "Independent" reported that Ireland is a major route for trafficking children doomed to a life of slavery or prostitution in Britain. Ireland, like several other countries involved in slavery and the slave trade serves as a transit, center for buying and selling slaves and for export.

"The exact number of slaves in Ireland can never be determined, although they run in tens of thousands. They are there; slaves are there undoubtedly," Senator Mullen told the Independent daily.

In keeping with the main aim of presenting an objective work devoid of any pernicious information, the news concerning slavery and acts related to slavery are reflected as they have appeared in original text form.

Writer John Martin writing on "The Irish Slave Trade—The Forgotten White Slaves" stated: "They came as slaves; vast human cargo transported on tall British ships bound for the Americas. They were shipped by the hundreds of thousands and included men, women, and even the youngest of children."

It was not only the docile Africans transported to the Americas and enslaved, some in a cruel manner. In ancient times, the Greeks did this to the Greeks, the French did this to the French and even the British did this to the British and to the people of Scotland.

Recorded History and research from various dependable sources tells us that "Irish slaves in the New World" began when James II who ruled briefly between 1685-1688, ordered tens of thousand of Irish prisoners be sold as slaves to the New World. Ireland thus became the biggest source of slaves for English merchants. Not the African, but the Irish became the majority of early slaves in New World.

Substantiated research states that between 1641 and 1652, the English butchered an estimated half a million Irish in wars and skirmishes and captured alive a similar figure who were immediately sold as slaves. Ireland's population drastically fell by half within five years. The king decreed the prevention of Irish prisoners from taking their wives and children with them across the Atlantic. Such an act created untold miseries for women and children. This led to a helpless population of homeless women and children. Social problems afflicting the common Irish household increased.

Today, one needs to take a casual walk in the main streets of Dublin or to read cryptic advertisements in the local papers dealing with the supply of newly arrived entertainers, nannies and baby-sitters for a nominal fee. These messages deal with none but teenage girls with doctored identity papers trafficked for sale. An in-depth study into these horrifying advertisements leads ultimately to British, Arab, German and French brokers who buy these young girls and transport them to their final destinations of misery and destruction.

Until the year 2012, the Dublin Railway station served as a meeting place for brokers and suppliers of human cargo. Strangely enough, these brokers and suppliers were driven off the area only to meet in Cafes and Restaurants. While this trade in human flesh is not new in Ireland, only in very rare case there is an arrest. In case there is some form of indictment, the criminal is set free after some warning!

Various Societies assisting in freeing the young victims state that nearly all these young girls were simply eager to travel to another country for no valid reason; just the urge. Promise of jobs as baby-sitters, provider for the elderly, cleaning, restaurant server and telephone operators in a distant country simply excited them. None had their travel documents with them. All claimed their traffickers seized them. A nun in Dublin requesting anonymity said that at least half of those freed had some form of venereal and skin disease.

The Irish Government is considering legislation that would criminalize men for buying sex rather than women for selling it and this might go some way towards confronting the problem. This approach has halved street prostitution in a decade in Sweden and concrete results appear encouraging.

By the end of 2013, there were no indications that the saga of horror for young girls from various countries brought into Ireland has lessened.

Lithuania

> "If you run from a wolf, you may run into a bear."
>
> Lithuanian proverb.

Before going forward to examine the situation of slavery in "Lietuvos Respublika," (Republic of Lithuania) it is but justifiable to visit the historical grandeur of this once very large country; perhaps, among the largest in the world at that time.

In 1230s, the Lithuanian lands, was united by Mindaugas who was crowned as the Grand Duchy of Lithuania, the largest country in Europe. The Duchy extended from the Baltic coast to the western region of Ukraine.

During the Second World War, Russians ransacked The National Museum of Lithuania and the National Art Gallery in Vilnius. The Jewish Museums in Vilnius and Kaunas also were victims to Soviet robbery. The occupiers also emptied the Banks to their last silver and gold coins.

The reason for reflecting the above details is to convey this simple message; that the theft and outright robbery of Lithuania at that time by other countries has been responsible to a certain extent for creating hardships and poverty at a later period. England, France, the Netherlands, and Portugal looted their colonies of their wealth. The pangs of misery, hunger, poverty and instability are felt now because of what happened to these lands in the yesteryears.

Like Russia, Lithuania is also described as a source, transit and destination for women and children for the purpose of commercial sexual slavery. That also includes slavery in every conceivable form.

The U.S. State Department Trafficking in Persons Report in June 2009 said that approximately 20 percent of the victims are adolescent girls. Lithuanian women are trafficked within the country and to the United Kingdom, Germany, the Netherlands, Greece, Italy, France and the Czech Republic for the purpose of forced prostitution. Women from Belarus are trafficked to Lithuania for the same purpose. The end result of such deeds lead to slavery where the victim is often in bondage until he or she dies. The report also said that traffickers linked to organized crime in Europe were targeting boarding schools for orphans or from broken homes.

One shocking example of kidnapping and child slavery was accessed on February 18, 2011 in an article presented by Chris Bond of the Yorkshire Press, England, originally written on November 15, 2007. Mr. Bond's article created a lot of soul-searching within the British Parliament as to whether England had become a hub of slavery and whether the government has or will take any effective steps against this misery. It related to a fifteen-year-old young girl, only identified as "Danielle," with doctored documents from Lithuania, kidnapped to England by traffickers upon the promise of selling ice cream in the summer and earning some three hundred Pounds per month. The report said: "She was flown to Gatwick and sold in a coffee shop from one trafficker to another for Three Thousand Pounds! She was taken to a flat in London and forced into a life of prostitution with her owner making a substantial amount." Reports flowing out of London claimed that this young underage girl was enslaved between mid 2007 and late 2011. Subsequently, she found herself in the streets with her passport in a bag tied around her neck.

In October 2005, shocking news rocked the British Parliament when Judge Barber sentenced traffickers for trading in underage girls from Lithuania. Judge Barber referring to the traffickers said: "Their behavior absolutely beggared belief; they had taken two Lithuanian girls and transported them to Sheffield like cattle before putting them into a life of forced prostitution." The Crown Prosecution Service of England successfully prosecuted and sentenced to lengthy prison term Viktoras Larcenko, convicted of trafficking and trading in young and underage Lithuanian girls in England.

Agence France-Presse in February 26, 2006 reported that the number of young Lithuanian women including underage girls traded and even auctioned for sex in England has increased from "single cases to dozens every month," quoting the head of Lithuania's Interpol Bureau.

The much-respected Human Trafficking Foundation, based in England with branches in various major countries in Europe in late 2011 presented a harrowing report of slavery in England. The report said, "Most of the young and underage girls in England number more than ten thousand. Twice that figure in adult women bought and sold are from Greece, Turkey, Czech Republic, Slovakia, Lithuania, Latvia, Estonia, Romania, Bulgaria and Ukraine. Most of the crime rings operate in London"

Documents prove that one in eight slaves in the entire world is in Europe. In England alone, the underage girls in slavery and bondage exceed the ten thousand mark. The most pulverizing news is that today there are more slaves in the world than in the entire 350 years of the slave trade.

A spokesperson for the Human Trafficking Foundation requesting anonymity claimed that the figure of underage girls bought and traded and even auctioned into slavery in England increased by at least two thousand since the past three years. This increase has been noted beginning 2009, due to abyssal poverty and living standards in the Baltic States, Greece and Turkey where the girls are originally from. Gangs of traffickers have divided the regions between them; and in many instances have resorted to violence to settle feuds. Almost all their victims are teenage girls.

Once inside the country, the agents of the traffickers take all the travel documents and belongings of the victims. Organized crimes involved in trafficking human beings for slave labor, prostitution and bondage change their agents once every few months. They are rotated so as not to be identified by law enforcement authorities in whichever country and city they operate. A human smuggler once operating in London was traced to the same business in Lyons, France, while one operating as the chief of a trafficking ring in Vilnius, Lithuania, was found working in Tallinn, Estonia.

Just as in most of the countries of the world, there are no accurate numbers of underage girls being trafficked out of Lithuania to live as slaves for sexual exploitation. True figures are not available, unless any one of them die and are returned for burial to their home country or are registered as a deceased individual with proper identification. This would take several decades and usually with the death of one, thrice or more that many are new arrivals to lead this horrendous life.

Switzerland

"I prefer liberty with danger than peace with slavery."

Jean Jacques Rousseau

According to documents released by Human Trafficking and Modern-day Slavery, Switzerland is primarily a destination and, to a lesser extent, a transit country for women and children trafficked for the purposes of commercial sexual exploitation and forced labor. One Non-governmental Organization based in Geneva reported that roughly 50 percent of the trafficked victims counseled in Switzerland came from Eastern Europe, 27 percent were from South America; 14 percent from Asia; and the remaining 9 percent came from Africa.

A Human Rights report in 2006 stated that young girls have been kidnapped and trafficked from Poland, Czech Republic, Slovakia, Bulgaria, Russia, Ukraine, Lithuania, Latvia, Estonia and Belarus to serve the needs of the rich, mostly German, Austrian and French citizens who own costly homes in Switzerland. Since purchase of villas and homes are restricted to non-Swiss residents, the properties are usually purchased through an intermediary, usually a foreigner with Swiss residential permit. Nearly all the traffickers have been identified as Russians, Ukrainians, Poles and Romanians.

The girls are usually kept there to serve the pleasures of the person who has paid for the home and his guests, for a year or two and then replaced. The victims are then taken to the nearest border and left there to their fate and destiny.

Switzerland, through ages has been the bastion of courage and the greatest voice against slavery, sexual-exploitation of women and forced labor. Both Swiss men and women have vigorously fought this evil, not only in Switzerland but also abroad through the formation of several organizations and groups. In recent years, another Swiss has taken upon this mantle, this time, by Jacqueline Thibault, an uncompromising figure against slavery and exploitation of women who founded Fondation Surgir (the Arise Foundation) in Lausanne in early 2001.

Thibault has led a relentless crusade to battle the violence against women worldwide. Thibault, who is also the President of the Foundation, said that thousands of women trapped in forced marriages in Switzerland are suffering severe mental and physical abuse. Her Foundation cum Charity, which carried out the survey, is now calling up a national strategy to aid victims. Announcing the findings in Geneva on December 6, 2006, Thibault described the scale of the problems as "enormous." She added that many victims were too afraid to escape forced marriages for fear of reprisals.

The Canadian Broadcasting Corporation, CBC on May 19, 2006 reported that Switzerland has announced that it is replacing its entire Embassy and Consular staff in Pakistan after accusations some employees were involved in human trafficking racket. The other news related to Swiss Consular employees in the Visa section of the Swiss Embassy in Islamabad where applicants were sexually harassed.

Isobel Leybold reported in the "Swissinfo" on January 13, 2004 that cabaret dancers, mostly from Brazil, in Geneva, Zurich and Berne would still face violence and sexual exploitation, despite attempts to improve their lot, according to several women's groups based in Switzerland. Official reports by the government said that between twelve hundred and fifteen hundred women, mostly from Brazil and East Europe come to the country, on short-term permits to work in Switzerland's four hundred cabaret clubs.

Investigations by Prokore, an umbrella group for organizations lobbying for improved rights for sex workers, said that abuses including dishonesty over payments, violence and sexual exploitation were still rife.

The exact number of sex-slaves and other types of slavery in Switzerland is a murky subject. Despite the years of investigation and arrests, mostly of the traffickers and agents, who are mainly from the Balkan, the Baltic States and Russia, there appears to be ample number of women to replace them in case they escape the ordeal. It has been suggested that there are at least a hundred or so enslaved people, but they are mostly undocumented citizens of the Balkan States held in slave-like conditions by their own fellow compatriots who are official residents of Switzerland and are difficult to be identified. Save for the stray incident at the Swiss Consulate in Islamabad, Pakistan, no other incidents have been ever observed where a Swiss Citizen was either directly or indirectly involved in this gruesome trade.

Investigation by several Women's Association based in Switzerland as well as Anti-Slavery International have concluded that Swiss law enforcement officials as well as politicians have shown a very keen interest in vigorously fighting this atrocious trade and in bringing traffickers, agents and kidnappers to justice. Undoubtedly, they have been accomplishing this task at a very remarkable speed.

As early as April 2012, several dozens of traffickers who have been arrested during the past several years were found to be still imprisoned. A source from the United Nations praised the Swiss department of Justice and Police from refusing to show any form of leniency to such criminals. If any country has shown the willingness and the will to fight this menace, only Switzerland could be named. The Swiss people have individually commenced their own war against this terrible crime against humanity.

NORTH AMERICA

The United States of America

> "Americans are so enamored of equality that they be rather equal in slavery than unequal in freedom."
>
> Alexis de Tocqueville

There is a great degree of disagreement as to where and at which point the History of the United States of America should commence; the period when this land was snatched from the Natives or at the time when it officially became a colony of the British Empire, before that, or, immediately after the settlers had grown in a large number and could confront the Natives to a degree where they could slaughter the docile and "ever-believing" Natives and to gradually deprive them of their culture and customs, their lifestyle, their diet and even their beliefs.

Events related to slavery, could be more officially documented, from the time when the first ship bearing slaves arrived in Jamestown in 1619 in a Dutch Man-of-War, a frigate, bearing some twenty Africans. Research has shown that these slaves were probably seized as a prize from a slave trader bound for America. Initially identified as indentured servants these people were officially called slaves in 1656 henceforth, and in the 1660s, laws were created dealing with slaves and their position in society. Those laws were not meant to protect the individual slave in any way or form but to suggest punishments of various forms. Some of the punishments laid down were beatings, hangings and executions by firing. That year (1656) was the beginning of 247 years of combined slavery in the land now called the Spanish West Indies.

All historical documents and research, point to this fact that the settlers first enslaved the Natives through various ploys and craftiness, often citing their holy scriptures and interpreting the verses as god's will that non-believers obey the believers. The unaware and less educated Natives obliged, only to find themselves enslaved and in chains where their basic rights would be exploited and trampled by those holding the "book" in their hands as their license and permit to enslave the Natives whom they considered as savages unfit to lead a normal life, but born and created to serve the settlers!

A close look at the political elite of the United States Government tells an appalling tale of Presidents owning slaves. Between the years 1789 when George Washington was officially elected as the first President of the United States until the year 1877 when Ulysses Grant left office, there were eighteen such presidents.

The main point of discussion at this point is to state this fact that albeit, some of the Presidents mentioned were "African" by ethnic definition, they, not only rejected their own identity as having African blood, but, indulged in slavery and slave ownership.

Of the eighteen, twelve of them owned slaves and eight owned slaves even when they were President of the United States. Notable among those who owned slaves were George Washington, Thomas Jefferson, James Madison, James Monroe, Andrew Jackson, Martin Van Buren, William Henry Harrison, John Tyler, James Polk, Zachary Tyler, Andrew Johnson and Ulysses Grant. A total of eight of them continued to have slaves even after taking the office of the President.

Notorious among them who owned slaves while holding office of the President of the United States of America and until the end of their lives were:

George Washington owned two hundred and sixteen slaves by 1786. He served as President between 1789 and 1797.

Thomas Jefferson, President, 1801-1809, considered by many unread individuals as being a "gentleman President" and embellished with a "halo" of super human glory in good deeds was perhaps the largest slave owner in Virginia at one point. His wife brought him a dowry of more than a hundred slaves while he himself had nearly one hundred and forty one. In 1790, he gave his newly married daughter and her husband a thousand acres of land and twenty-five slaves. He never freed any of his slaves in his will.

James Madison, President (1809-1817) grew up in a slave owning family and owned slaves all his life. Sixteen years after the end of his second term as the President (1833), he sold sixteen slaves to a relative. He too, did not free his slaves in his will.

James Monroe, President (1817-1825), owned between thirty and forty slaves. He did not free his slaves in his will.

Andrew Jackson, President (1829-1837) owned about one hundred and sixty slaves. He did not free any of his slaves in his will.

John Tyler, President (1841-1845) did definitely have slaves but the accurate figure is unknown.

James Polk, President (1845-1849) is said to have fifteen slaves in 1832. Abolitionists criticized him for being an instrument of "Slave Power." His father, Samuel Polk left him with more than eight thousand acres of land and fifty-three slaves, which was divided between his widow and his children. Polk inherited a good number and had his own slaves too. His will stipulated that all slaves be freed after the death of his wife, but in 1865, the Thirteenth Amendment to the United States Constitution freed all slaves, long before the death of his wife Sarah in 1891.

Zachary Taylor, President (1849-1850) owned more than a hundred slaves in 1847 until his death in 1850.

Ulysses Grant, President (1869-1877) did own slaves, but the exact number is unknown. The only evidence that he owned slaves is a document he signed in 1859 freeing one slave named William Jones. Nevertheless, he is not included as a President owning slaves while holding office.

Of these Presidents, two identified as having African roots; Thomas Jefferson and Andrew Jackson, had slaves before and at the time of holding the office of the President of the United States and even after that. None of them freed their slaves in their will.

One finds it a challenge to even comprehend the reasons and philosophy of this socially arcane passion of owning slaves, keeping them, and vaunting them to reflect their status-quo as a dominator, even though holding the highest office in the United States of America, that of a President.

Once the picture of American-slavery in the past among the elites is understood, the harrowing developments related to modern-day slavery in the United States of America would not come as a shock.

Documents related to Human Trafficking and Modern-day Slavery in the United States of America, prepared by the Central Intelligence Agency's report of 2008, estimated the number of people trafficked or transited through the United States of America annually, as sex-slaves, domestics (the enslaved), garment and agricultural slaves, at fifty thousand people.

The United States State Department Trafficking in Persons Report of June 2009 quoted a slight larger figure, in comparison to those released by the Central Intelligence Agency. In none of the reports made public is there a total figure, or even an approximate figure of those either enslaved or working in slave-like conditions, whether sex-slaves or forced labor.

The respected "Polaris Project," an Organization combating Human Trafficking and Modern-day Slavery, which also serves to rehabilitate rescued victims of slavery claims that at any given time there are over a hundred thousand children in the sex-trade in the United States each year. Parents against Child Exploitation, a small group of concerned parents based in California, said the figure is higher and is increasing at an alarming rate. The report states that the United States is a destination country for thousands of men; women and children trafficked largely from Mexico and East Asia as well as countries in South Asia, Central America, Africa and Europe, for the purposes of sexual and labor exploitation.

Most of the trafficking is done from the southern borders of Mexico, which is either poorly monitored or very porous. Most of the victims work in agriculture chiefly in pig-farms, corn and wheat fields in slave-like conditions for paltry payments.

Many young girls smuggled in from the southern borders, are not originally from Mexico but from Costa Rica, Argentina, Panama, Nicaragua, Honduras, Guatemala, El Salvador, Dominican Republic, Brazil and even Haiti. They serve as sex-slaves for the affording individual, mostly US citizens, but originally from Honduras, Mexico, Panama, Cuba or Costa Rica. Almost all of the victims are devoid of any identification papers and live in confinement in luxurious homes. Nearly all of the enslavers have a history of crime or are involved in unlawful acts, drugs and other crimes.

One of the recent most tragedies to afflict the USA and Canada is the open sale of Native American women, children and infants. They were earlier trafficked from various parts of the United States of America and Canada and brought to a holding area on board abandoned freighters moored alongside jetties on Lake Superior between Thunder Bay, Ontario, Canada and Duluth, Minnesota, USA. Residents of Duluth harbor claim that the harbor region is infamous for the numerous abandoned freighters where Native women and children are always for sale.

It is a known fact that there are dozens of groups of Chinese businesspersons each operating several Chinese Restaurants in any one Province throughout Canada. These groups also own Chinese Restaurants in the United States of America. The larger percentage of their employees are Chinese citizens smuggled into Canada where after working for a few years are again smuggled into the US to serve in the "US Branch" Restaurants.

The northern borders with Canada also appear porous and unmanned for hundreds of miles at a stretch thus facilitating traffickers from Canada into smuggling in young women from Eastern Europe to cater to the needs of a variety of people in the United States of America. The girls are virtually from every corner of the world. The young women do have documents; mostly doctored ones to identify them as adults.

Young Ukrainian, Romanian, Russian, Czech and Slovak girls are smuggled into the USA through Canada. They are first sold to agents in Canada before they even enter there, and in turn sold to the agents from the USA. They are the sex-slaves. Their numbers are unknown but believed to be in the thousands every year. Most of them are beaten and escape back to Canada from the same porous borders.

In mid 2010, reports from various sources including the major television channels revealed a humongous figure of up to eleven and a half million undocumented foreigners living in the United States of America. Many other news sources reported the true figure to exceed sixteen million. Several conservative channels suggest a grossly exaggerated figure of twenty million illegal workers.

The figure of eleven and a half million is approximate and identifies more than six million working in various capacities where skilled labor is not required. The skilled labor work force that is not easily visible could be at least five million and is mostly concentrated in urban areas where the individual has means of proper accommodation. Both the skilled and the unskilled illegal workers receive less than half the amount paid to the citizens of the country.

The CBS, ABC, NBC and the CNN channels showed instances where tens of thousands of laborers, mostly from the Central and Southern part of the American Continent are engaged in slave-labor under the most grueling conditions in the country, chief among them; California, Texas, Ohio, Idaho, Utah, New Mexico, Arizona, Oklahoma and Florida. The Networks showed very young workers in cattle and pig-farms and struggling under the heat growing vegetables. Many are also employed in tanneries, meatpacking, garment factories and even privately owned mines with sub-standard safety conditions.

At regular intervals, the mass media in the United States of America reports the unbearable situation in garment factories and sweatshops where young children trafficked from several Central and South American countries are working. Many have been pictured fallen asleep due to fatigue or have simply fainted due to stress of working very long hours a day. Their payments do not exceed a dollar with some unwholesome sandwich for the entire work period, sometimes exceeding sixteen hours. These production units are not registered and are mostly in the countryside, far from the prying eyes of the law.

In major cities like New York, Los Angeles, Chicago, Houston and elsewhere forced child labor is employed in garment manufacturing units, mostly located in dilapidated homes where dozens of child workers are crammed in small rooms with space enough for an outdated electrically operated sewing machine.

The "Polaris Project" has numbered the unfortunate child slave-laborers to number in tens of thousands! People contact this Organization in the United States for a variety of reason; to help them find their missing children, who may have become victims of trafficking and enslavement or, if dead, to find their place of burial. The subject of tracking and following slavery in its various forms in the United States of America is a cumbersome task with no definite answers. Statistics are often vague, conflicting and even self-serving.

Most of the Rescue and Aid Organizations, Groups and Societies helping in the freedom of enslaved victims have sprung up on their own, chiefly due to the altruistic reflections of the majority of the citizens of the United States of America. Many, perhaps, a hundred thousand and more have been rescued from their miseries, enslavement and horrors flung upon them by fellow human beings.

During the past quarter century, the administration of President Bill Clinton made serious efforts to track down traffickers and to deal them a heavy blow. Hundreds of traffickers and their immediate seniors were arrested, tried and sentenced, only to be replaced by even a larger number.

Immediately after Clinton, the administration of George W. Bush continued to relentlessly hunt the traffickers. Other exigencies during his presidency weakened the fight against trafficking and smuggling of human beings into the country.

President Obama's administration took on the case with greater vigor and determination and managed to weaken human trafficking through both the Canadian and the Mexican borders. The victimizers found other porous borders and routes to smuggle in men, women and children to be employed as slaves with just a meager amount not exceeding two dollars a day together with a few morsels of bread. They were smuggled in tunnels, some with a length of a kilometer from one side of the border to the other side!

From the northern borders of Canada, most of those smuggled into the United States were well to do, mostly Chinese, Russian and Koreans. They paid a hefty amount to be smuggled through the various routes, each belonging to a specific group of human smuggling ring.

From the Southern borders of Mexico, mostly poor people from several Central and South American countries paid their entire belongings to smugglers to be transported to the United States. Many were arrested, some even died in the journey. Once inside the country, they were employed by farmers and ranch owners through agents. Immediately upon employment, these people became slaves.

In case a profound study is made in relation with slavery and enslavement in the United States of America, dozens of volumes would not suffice.

Mexico

> "In the end they will lay their freedom at our feet and say to us,
> make us your slave, but feed us."
>
> Fyodor Dostoyevsky

Slavery was universal in Mexico even before the arrival of the European settlers. Theoretically, with the arrival of the Europeans, that should have changed.

In an article written by Shep Lenchek, European settlers, condoned as well as forbid slavery, but that related to a certain group and class of people.

Queen Isabella of Spain in 1500 decreed, "All the Indians of the Spaniards were to be free from slavery." This was a direct order without any clauses attached.

In 1493, Pope Alexander VI while granting Spain the right to colonize the New World, mandated that the indigenous people be converted to

Catholicism and prohibited their enslavement. However, in his message, he entered a clause that in case the natives refused to accept Christianity or reverted to their old faith, they should be punished and enslaved.

Four years later in 1504, after the death of Queen Isabella of Spain, controversies and conflict of interpretation of the Royal decree once again introduced slavery in the Central and Southern hemisphere of the New World. Since then, slavery in a variety of forms existed in the larger part of Mexico whose territories also included present day California, Utah, Nevada, Arizona, New Mexico and elsewhere (Mexican cession of 1848) till the year 1820, when slavery was abolished throughout Mexico based upon the Plan of Iguala proposed of General Augustin de Iturbide.

The U.S. State Department Trafficking in Persons Report of June 2009 stated that Mexico is a large source, transit, and destination country for persons trafficked for the purposes of commercial sexual exploitation and forced labor. Groups considered most vulnerable to human trafficking in Mexico include women and children, indigenous persons, and undocumented migrants.

It is no secret that at least fifty thousand people from the porous and unguarded borders of Mexico are trafficked annually into the United States of America, ostensibly for the purpose of sexual enslavement and forced labor. Most of the young girls trafficked end up as prostitutes. Some, prior to their arrival on U.S. soil, are sold to affording individuals with their pictures as the commodity for sale.

"Trafficked victims are usually from the rural areas of Mexico and are often from broken families and very poor, and are tricked into being taken safely into any State within the United States of America for a better life and future," said a journalist from the popular and dependable "Atlanta Constitution" who requested anonymity.

The victims are as young as twelve and thirteen and are often kidnapped. Prior to the kidnappings and later trafficking, the traffickers photograph the unaware underage girls and send their pictures to prospective buyers in the United States. Some are however, bought from their parents who are poor. Once the victim is smuggled across the Mexican border into the United States, instead of being taken to their promised work place are handed to other agents inside the U.S. border and from there, delivered to the doorstep of the person who has ordered the girl. The owners are mostly people from any one of the Central or South American countries who use the underage girls as sex-slaves until such a time the she needs to be replaced.

Not all the underage girls smuggled into the United States are from Mexico. They are from other Central and South American countries; Panama, Costa Rica, El Salvador, Ecuador, Paraguay, Venezuela, Brazil, tricked into going to the United States for prosperity and a better life. Some are trafficked for thousands of kilometers until they arrive at their destinations. Every few hundred kilometers, the agent in charge is changed to further confuse the already emotionally and mentally beclouded young victim. At intervals, the victim is sexually assaulted.

It has been suggested but not confirmed, that the majority of victims from Brazil are the young shemales; exported for the pleasures of rich Americans. An unconfirmed report claimed that the young shemales were housed in posh villas away from the prying eyes of the public. The shemales were to serve not only the owner but also the owner's guests and friends.

Emilio Godoy writing for the Inter Press Service in a report dated August 13, 2007 but accessed only on February 20, 2011, said that virtually all the International Organizations fighting child sex tourism claim that Mexico is one of the leading hotspots for child sexual exploitation along with Thailand, Cambodia, India and Brazil.

Reports from social workers reflected a chilling statistic that 95 percent of Mexico City's street children have already had at least one sexual encounter with an adult.

Sally Kalson, writing in the Pittsburgh Post Gazette on June 5, 2006 gave a gruesome picture of the aftermaths of slave labor in Pittsburgh, a city of nearly a million and half inhabitants that includes the various large suburbs. In the report, she said, "a number of U.S. companies built plants around Pittsburgh to take advantage of low-cost Mexican labor after the 1993 passage of the North American Free Trade Agreement."

A United Nations' report dated January 26, 2005 and accessed on September 8, 2011 claimed that some three hundred twenty young women were the victims of unsolved murders in Ciudad Juarez, near the U.S. border, between January 1993 and July 2003. Suggested motives were trafficking in organs and for sexual exploitation.

An article accessed on September 8, 2011 from the American Family Journal and originally written on April 15, 2004 spoke of harrowing developments in the sex-slave trade in the United States of America.

The writer identified as "Hughes" wrote that "virtual sex is not the only decadent delicacy for some Americans; the simple fact is that thousands of trafficked women and girls are ferried into the U.S. for the purpose of sexual encounters and slavery." Hughes also wrote about the extent of the sex trafficking industry that shuttles girls through Mexico to brothels outside San Diego, California.

Mexico also serves as a transit point for very young girls who are trafficked to Japan. The Associated Press on April 29, 2005 gave an alarming report that the Japanese sex industry, including organized crime, namely the "Yakuza" annually place large orders for young girls from Mexico, Peru, Ecuador, El Salvador and Venezuela. More than a thousand persons are employed as traffickers by smugglers and agents operating through "private companies" to escape detection. It is easy to obtain travel documents for a nominal bribe to the Mexican authorities, and smuggle the young victims out of Mexican airports. Persons often accompany the underage girls with falsified documents posing as the father of three or four girls at any single time. Their Tokyo destination is supposedly for tourism.

There is no indication as to the fate and destiny of the trafficked young girls at any given time. Complaints by family members to their own governments have no effect. Records show none returned to their families, whether in Mexico, Peru, Ecuador, El Salvador or Venezuela. The several announcements made in local newspapers in various cities of these countries about the missing girls prove this fact. After years, there is little explanation either from the Interior Ministries or from the National Police of these countries, especially Mexico.

Meanwhile, local organization aided by concerned citizens from the cities of the disappeared persons, mainly young girls continue to search for the victim of kidnapping, unaware that organized crime groups are behind the abductions, kidnapping and trafficking of human beings.

Mexico continues to be one of the worst places on earth in terms of lawlessness, murder and human kidnappings. Topping the list is India.

CENTRAL AND SOUTH AMERICA

Federative Republic of Brazil

> "The moment the slave resolves that he will no longer be a
> slave, his fetters fail. He frees himself and shows the way to
> others. Freedom and slavery are mental states."
>
> Mahatma Gandhi

Brazil has always been considered as a beacon of economic development
and prosperity in the southern hemisphere of the American Continent.
Wealth and abject poverty has nevertheless walked besides the two
distinct classes of society.

The U.S. State Department Trafficking in Persons Report in June 2009
stated that Brazil is a source country for men, women, girls and boys
trafficked within the country and trans-nationally for the purpose of
commercial sexual exploitation, as well as a source country for men and
boys trafficked internally for forced labor.

The Brazilian Federal Police estimate that at any given time at least
half a million children are exploited in domestic prostitution, in resort
and tourist areas, along highways and in Amazonian mining brothels.
Prominent freelance journalist Gabrielle Pickard compiled parts of this
investigative report on the prevailing conditions of slavery in Brazil.

According to the United Nations report on slavery in Brazil, it noted
that Brazilians are the major victims of international human trafficking.
Most victims are women aged between eighteen and thirty with a low
educational background.

Ms. Gulnara Shahinian, Special Rapporteur on Contemporary Forms
of Slavery in Brazil believes that loopholes in the current legal system
of Brazil are disabling the progression of wiping out slavery in Brazil. A
virtual absence of criminal penalties and jurisdictional conflicts in the
judiciary system result in slavery flourishing in many rural regions of
Brazil. A part of the report stated that the victims of forced labor work for

long hours, with little or no pay. They are threatened with or subjected to physical, psychological and sometimes sexual violence.

UNICEF's Ms. Alison Sutton, based in the Brazilian capital Brasilia, who authored a book about slavery in Brazil, reiterates Ms. Shahinian's beliefs that better education of the rural workers in Brazil is the real solution to combat this depraved practice.

In a report to the United Nations, Ms. Shahinian stressed, "The strongest message that the Brazilian government can send is to pass the constitutional amendment which would allow for the expropriation of land where forced labor and slavery is used."

Brazil's ascendency into the soon to be the "fifth biggest economy in the world" is arguably having a detrimental effect on the rights of people and is explicitly breeding slavery.

Many anti-capitalists believe that capitalist economic systems are responsible for breeding slavery. Mr. Steve Butler from the United Kingdom is of this line of thought commenting: "Capitalism, by its very nature, breeds slavery. If you want to end slavery you have to come up with a better economic system than capitalism."

One of the worst forms of dehumanizing humankind takes place in Brazil. The other is Mexico, India, and to a lesser extent Thailand and to a negligible extent the Philippines. This pertains to changing the identity of a human being to what is commonly called the "third gender!"

Young homeless boys living in the streets in various major cities of Brazil; Rio de Janeiro, Brasilia, Sao Paolo and elsewhere are kidnapped and taken to a center specially created for them by human traffickers for a very special form of slavery; to turn them into a "travesti;" a she male or a transsexual to earn money for the owners, which is in fact the most abject form of disgrace to mankind.

At this point, it is but befitting to say that this cruelty is also done with abandoned children in the Kingdom of Thailand and in parts of the Philippines. There, they are given the title of a "ladyboy!" The destiny of that young boy turned into a "third gender" at an early age is known for at least the time the victim is twenty-five or a bit more. After that, the victim simply vanishes. There is no further news about his life.

A report prepared upon the instructions of Judge Whitaker; the President of the Sub-Committee of Human Rights in Geneva in the year 1984, reported several dead bodies hurriedly cremated outside the city limits of Bangkok as that of "human beings having genitals with breast implants." The Bangkok Police denied any such thing due to the absence of proof by way of pictures. Five badly burned corpses were said to have been counted. The report also said that there were no individuals in the vicinity to claim any form of relation with the funeral pyres.

All said, enslaved "ladyboys" number in the thousands in Thailand and their main place of business is in Pattaya and Bangkok. Independent investigative reports also claim that very young boys are smuggled into Thailand from Cambodia, Vietnam, the Philippines, China and Myanmar and transformed into the "third gender."

In Brazil, there are several dozens of groups of kidnappers involved in this explicit trade. In order to mask their trade, these groups function as business companies under various names, dealing with artistic renditions and human art works, which are virtually impossible to either identify or even prosecute.

The kidnappers abduct these homeless and abandoned children in the streets, and drive them to secret places where they classify the children as very desirable, just desirable or undesired. The undesired ones are transported to regions and sold to agents requiring young boys for slave labor. Of note is that the centers usually change address to evade any form of problem with the law or investigative journalists. The desirable and the just desirable are transferred to a more permanent place, usually on the outskirts of the city for further processing.

The term "processing" refers to the commencement of a sex-slave life for these voiceless children for the next few months where the business owners sexually assault them in turns. They undergo this misery until they appear a bit grown up and are deemed fit to have "breast augmentation" surgery and used in the sex trade. At that moment, after the surgery, the victim transforms into "travesti" or a transvestite who can now earn money for the company, which in reality means criminal enslavers. Entering such a stage in life spells a point of no return for them whose identity is fully changed. They are a "she" as well as a "he" both in one! The victims are often given a "melodious" female name, which they never change until the end of their lives.

Investigations have shown that this form of assault on mankind's dignity has been going on in Brazil at least for the last fifty years. Some reports claim it is more than a century.

Sexual services rendered by "she males" in Brazil earn the owners hundreds of millions in the equivalent of US dollars each year. Pornographic films turn in at least a hundred million dollars each year.

A member of the Brazilian Embassy in Washington requesting anonymity said that there are at least two hundred thousand of such dehumanized beings in the "third gender" in Brazil used in the sex trade, employing at least half a million people in various businesses related to their activities. Their maximum age is twenty-nine while investigations have unearthed victims as young as twelve.

What is very sad about this episode is that after the victims arrive at a certain age where their body does not any longer have the desired sexual appeal to customers, they are discarded. A discreet investigation by the Ministry of Interior of Brazil in 2009 stated that they could not find any "she male" above the age of fifty. It is a very difficult procedure to undo the physical changes that they have been subjected to in the past. So where are they? What future does a human being with male genitals and breasts have?

Those designated as undesired children picked up in the major cities and found unsuitable to be a "she male" have an equally doomed future. They die of various ailments and disease because of sexual exploitation, slave labor, undernourishment and beatings.

Meanwhile, more and more children are abandoned in the major cities of Brazil and newer faces of sexual victims of the "third gender" are entering the sex market.

Costa Rica and Nicaragua

> "Knowledge makes a man unfit to be a slave."
>
> Frederick Douglass

Most of the South American countries also referred to as "Spanish America" experience abyssal poverty, which in turn creates a lack of opportunity for proper education. This excludes Costa Rica with a stable economy, which depends on tourism, agriculture and electronic export. Venezuela's economy is marginally better when compared to most of the other nations north and south of it.

Nicaragua is principally a source and transit country for women and children trafficked for the purposes of commercial sexual exploitation and forced labor. Women and children are trafficked within the country and to neighboring countries, most often to El Salvador, Costa Rica, Guatemala, Honduras, Mexico, and to the United States.

Abject poverty and unemployment in Nicaragua has been a major factor for women and underage girls to enter a life of prostitution, either in the country or in neighboring countries. Internal trafficking is the exploitation of children, both boys and girls, in prostitution. Reports indicate that less than five thousand people are involved in slave labor in Nicaragua.

Nicaragua, El Salvador, Ecuador, Peru, Paraguay, Uruguay and Panama have faltering economies. At certain times, the unemployment rate is unbearable, leading to desperation, which in the end paves way for slave labor and prostitution.

All the above named countries indulge in internal slavery, although on a lower scale, but trafficking and smuggling young boys and girls into Mexico, some to be ultimately trafficked to the United States of America through several corridors is of serious concern since a good percentage of the abductees die in the long journey.

Nearly all the organizations involved in fighting slavery have given a uniform report for Central and South American countries; that the victims are kidnapped and sold into slavery; first within the national borders of that particular country, then sold to the country north of its borders and so on till they arrive at the Mexican border where gangs of traffickers await the victims through a prior appointment. From Mexico, they are sent to other countries, depending on the demands of organized crimes mostly located in Japan, South Korea, the U.S.A., parts of West Europe and even Saudi Arabia.

Unlike Nicaragua, Costa Rica also serves as a destination country for women and children trafficked for the purposes of commercial sex. U.S. State Department reports indicate that Costa Rica is a source, transit and destination country for men, women, and children trafficked into forced labor, particularly in agriculture, construction, restaurant work, fishing industry, and as domestic servants.

The U.S. Department of Labor Bureau of International Labor Affairs in 2005 claimed that Costa Rica is witnessing the worst forms of Child Labor. The report notes that the commercial sexual exploitation of children is a continuing problem in Costa Rica, and is often associated with the country's sex tourism industry. Costa Rica is a transit and destination point for children trafficked for purposes of commercial sexual exploitation, including prostitution. Most trafficking victims originate from Colombia, the Dominican Republic, Nicaragua, Panama, as well as from Russia, the Philippines, Romania, Eastern Europe, and Ecuador. Although most foreign victims remain in Costa Rica, traffickers also attempt to transport them onward to the U.S. and Canada.

The Paul H. Nitze School of Advanced International Studies and the John Hopkins University in a joint finding said that Costa Rica is believed to have the region's largest child prostitution problem. One report claims that annually, more than three thousand underage girls are prostituted in Costa Rica; many of them trafficked from Colombia, the Dominican Republic, Honduras, and Nicaragua. Almost all the underage children are bought from their parents and promised a good life in Costa Rica only to be exploited when they arrive. In turn, Costa Rican children are believed to be trafficked to other countries for sexual exploitation purposes as well.

CHAPTER III

ROLE OF RELIGION IN SLAVERY

"So many religions are there because so many people are unhappy. A happy person needs no religion; a happy person needs no temple, church—because for a happy person the whole universe is a temple, the whole existence is a church. The happy person has nothing like religious activity because his whole life is religious."

Osho

"This is my simple religion. There is no need for temples; no need for complicated philosophy. Our own brain, our own heart is our temple; the philosophy is kindness."

Dalai Lama

Religions, whether considered monotheistic or defined as otherwise are extensively blamed for either promoting or encouraging slavery. Justifications are often citied through the interpretation of verses from the Bible, the Torah or the Koran to indulge in this vile trade.

(Author)

Although no specific verses from any of these three writings directly encourage or condemn slavery, humankind has managed to relay murky messages to the common public suggesting the three divine books may have or possibly could have said things justifying slavery. No definite statements clearly relate any specific religion to condoning slavery.

Popular Journalist and writer John Blake of the CNN news channel in an article titled "Slavery's Last Stronghold" in an interview on March 29, 2012 questioned writer John D. Sutter about his views on "How religion has been used to promote slavery."

The main question was as to which revered religious figure—Moses, Jesus or the Prophet Mohammed spoke out boldly and unambiguously against slavery to which Sutter responded: "None of them! One of these men owned slaves, another created laws to regulate—but not ban—slavery." The Prophet of Islam's chief spokesperson even ordered slaves to obey their masters, religious scholars say.

The vast majority of followers of the three major religions condemn slavery as an essential evil. Many however, find loopholes to condone it as a will of the Creator!

"The lesson in all this is we need historical humility," says Daniel C. Peterson, author of "Muhammad, Prophet of God."

Scholars on theocracy and comparative religions have found it a very cumbersome task to find an appropriate and a straightforward answer. At best, the response to all these questions would be laced with errors and contradictions. Scholars of all the three religions agree that all the three founders may have deliberately ignored or even tolerated slavery in one form or the other.

Slavery in Christianity

John Dominic Crossan, the globally reputed Irish-American Bible scholar, in his views and methodology argued at length that the parables of Jesus, for example were full of reference to slaves and slavery. Terms like "servants" or "stewards" are what we would call as slaves today. He also said that; "Yet Jesus does not seem to make any moral judgments about slavery in his parables, nor did he ever say anything for or against it."

Crossan, the Jesus scholar, claimed that all his research showed that Jesus did not personally own any slaves and neither did any of his disciples or the crowds Jesus addressed. "They were all too poor and lived under desperate economic circumstances. Still, Jesus would have opposed slavery," Crossman insists.

At various parts of the New Testament, Paul who is widely believed to have never met Jesus seems to accept slavery. He tells slaves to obey their masters. In one way or the other, Paul also seems to contradict himself and challenges the morality of slavery. In a New Testament letter, Paul intercedes on behalf of a runaway slave and chides the master for calling himself a Christian and holding a slave.

Crossan, along with some other biblical scholars says there are actually two versions of Paul in the New Testament: the authentic, "radical" Paul who opposed slavery and a "Pseudo-Paul" inserted into the texts by early church leaders who were afraid of antagonizing Rome.

It is interesting to note that the American Christians who owned slaves had a simple but powerful defense in the run-up to the Civil War. The Old and the New Testament sanctioned slavery and, since the Bible is infallible, slavery is a part of God's order, says Mark Noll, author, "The Civil War as a Theological Crisis."

A good number of Fundamentalist Christian preachers in the United States of America suggest that every line of the Bible is to be followed without hesitation. This does not preclude the evils of slavery! Televangelists enslave their superstitious audience through the power of suggestion to part with a major portion of their income to "god" but through him. The audience responds accordingly. This is mind control and a form of slavery.

The church members are virtual slaves. Some of them go without proper food and clothing, but willingly donate to the wily preachers who have made it a business to invoke god while robbing the unaware and superstitious public. The audience volunteers to play the role of a slave while the preachers play their role as the "master of ceremonies" in the most professional manner, turning their followers into slaves with just a few words.

Almost all of the televangelist preachers live in opulence at the cost of the poor church members who are ever ready to part with whatever they have to please the foxy preacher. This is "voluntary slavery" by the public towards the individual claiming divinity. Some of the notorious Christian preachers promise a life full of bliss and rewards both while living and after death, if sufficient monetary contributions are made to them. They ask subjugation from their audience and the audience complies.

Slavery in Islam

Examining the Islamic side of this subject, scholars from the various denominations of Islam say that the Prophet Mohammed (Muhammad) never explicitly condemned slavery, and actually owned slaves.

Ali S. Asani, expert in comparative religions and author of "Celebrating Muhammad: Images of the Prophet in Popular Muslim Poetry" states that the Prophet never explicitly condemned slavery, yet he recognized the humanity of slaves, teaching followers that freeing slaves was an act of piety. He allowed slaves to buy their freedom and demanded that they should be treated with love and respect.

"He himself did own slaves but he treated them as family," Asani says. "One called Zayd, he treated like an adopted son and one of his wives was a Coptic Christian slave."

By the time of the crusades, Christians and Muslims were enslaving one another by the thousands. They cited their faith as justification, says Robert C, Davis, author of "Holy War and Human Bondage." Davis also states that, "One Pope said that the justification for slavery was that it was important for spreading the faith. Once they were enslaved, they would more readily take to Christianity."

Such actions and approaches vis-à-vis the prisoner in both sides of the crusades may now appear to be an act of brainwashing, mental torture and deprivation of freedom of thought and expression, which translates into a more profound form of slavery. Some of the infamous Muslim clergy threaten the public with god's wrath coupled with severe divine punishment for failing to obey his commands.

Nevertheless, the writings to justify slavery, albeit considered foreboding and evil, are printed in the sacred texts of Judaism, Christianity and Islam. It has been often argued by experts in Theology and Bible scholars, that today, very few people, if at all, would quote those scriptures favoring slavery and many even do not know that they exist.

"We should not be surprised," says Jonathan Brockopp, a religion professor at Pennsylvania State University. "Religions redefine themselves and people draw on different stories and underplay other stories. This happens constantly."

Slavery in Judaism

Jewish views on slavery are varied both religiously and historically. Judaism's religious texts contain numerous laws governing the ownership and treatment of slaves. The Tanakh (Hebrew Bible), and the Talmud (Instructions and text of Rabbinic Judaism) and the 12th century Mishneh Torah (Code of Jewish religious laws written by Rabbi Maimonides) and the Shulchan Aruch (Code of Jewish laws written by Rabbi Yosef Karo) all have different rules vis-à-vis the treatment of slaves. The Hebrew Bible contained two sets of laws, one for Cananite slaves and a more lenient law for Hebrew slaves. Like their Christian and Muslim neighbors, the Jewish people owned and traded in slaves.

The above statements add impetus to the fact that all the three major religions owned and traded in slavery.

Minor religions have consistently stood opposed to slavery. One example is the Baha'i faith.

Abu'l-Qasim Afnan, a prominent Baha'i scholar discusses the place of slavery in the book "Black Pearls: Notes on Slavery" quotes Baha'u'llah (Glory of God), founder of the Baha'i Faith where humanity's relations are concerned with slavery.

In his Most Holy Book, the Kitab-i Aqdas (1873), Baha'u'llah has written:

> "It is forbidden you to trade in slaves, be they men or women. It is not for him who is himself a servant to buy another of God's servants, and this hath been prohibited in His Holy Tablet. Thus, by His mercy, hath the commandment been recorded by the Pen of justice. Let no man exalt himself above another; all are but bond slaves before the Lord, and all exemplify the truth, that there is none other God but Him."

CHAPTER IV

WAR AGAINST SLAVERY

It would be morally and spiritually befitting to dedicate this chapter to the memory of Robert "Councillor" Carter III (1727-1804), who took the most courageous step ever in the history of slavery by freeing nearly five hundred slaves in 1787 soon after the demise of his wife, Frances Ann Task Carter, and after embracing the Swedenborgian faith. His manumission is the largest known release of slaves in North American history prior to the Civil War and the largest number ever manumitted by any individual in the United States of America.

> "We now live in a nation, where
> Doctors destroy health,
> Lawyers destroy justice,
> Universities destroy knowledge,
> Governments destroy freedom,
> The Press destroys information,
> Religion destroys morals,
> And our Banks destroy the economy."
>
> Christopher Lynn Hedges

One June 20, 2012, U.S. Secretary of State Hillary Clinton informed the world that up to twenty seven million people are living in slavery around the world today!

At the unveiling of the report at the State Department, she said, "The end of legal slavery in the United States and other countries around the world has not, unfortunately, meant the end of slavery." She added that the victims of modern day slavery are women and men, boys and girls, and their stories remind us of the kind of inhumane treatment we are capable of as human beings. Out of the 185 countries included in the 2012 report, only 33 complied fully with laws in place to end human trafficking.

As America prepares to mark the 150th anniversary of the proclamation of the emancipation of U.S. slaves, people must reflect on "how much further we have to go on to free all these twenty-seven million victims," Clinton added.

The figure of twenty-seven million is the American version of the number of slaves globally, but a more unbiased study of the subject of slavery and its various forms narrate to the common mind a different figure. The numbers of slaves, forced and slave-labor, and slave-like treatment including a variety of dungeon-like imprisonments in India, Pakistan, Bangladesh, China, North Korea, Iran, Saudi Arabia, Brazil, Mexico, the U.S.A., the whole of Europe, and the entire African continent present us a different figure. Undoubtedly, the figure of twenty-seven million is far below the actual figure.

Waging a war; in the right meaning of the word, to create harmony and liberation for mankind would be the most unheard type of war in the history of mankind. This would be a necessary war, a war, which will destroy chains, shackles, and fetters that have been around the body of human beings since time immemorial.

There are two parties in this episode; the oppressor and the oppressed; the dominator and the dominated. These are the only ones who need to be addressed. This war will not resort to guns and bullets. This war will not suggest bloodshed, although the victimizers have shed blood and snuffed out innocent lives. Unfolding this million years old business and disbanding the organizations involved is the main aim.

Mass scale education and enlightenment by allocation of budgetary considerations to aid the victim until a time that he or she no longer requires the crutches of society is of cardinal importance. The victimizer too, requires rehabilitation and tutoring towards a meaningful life until a stage where he or she could be the pride of the society. This solution will not come to fruition within days, months or even years. It will perhaps take more than a decade.

The war against slavery would in fact have global dimensions, which may eventually pit a neighboring country against the other, who may have had cordial relations; either as business partners or through some strategic cooperation in case one refuses to join hands in this global effort.

This means that all countries in between Chile in the southernmost tip of the American Continent to Canada in the north must be united and determined to drive away slavery from that part of the world. In the same vein, from China in the east of Asia until the British coast on the Atlantic, all nations between, must be dedicated and united to fight this menace. The same deals with each and every country in the African continent.

Not all the countries notorious for having slaves would comply with a global campaign to eradicate slavery. Outstanding among them would be countries where slavery is State-sponsored: the Theocratic Islamic Republic of Iran, China and North Korea. India, Pakistan, Bangladesh and Indonesia would prove to be very difficult regions to consider as volunteers to this war.

Waging an effective war against this multi-headed monster that has been haunting societies throughout the world is not an easy task. This ultimate monster will not perish and disappear on its own. It needs to be crushed and permanently crushed but with a correct tactic. This gargantuan task requires a dedicated, coordinated and cumulative effort against the joint forces of evil; be they individuals, groups, organized crime or State sponsored that are actively prevalent in several countries.

Public speeches from national or international podiums will have no effect until and unless a clarion call is made to all the participating nations to join hands in all honesty and deal a crushing blow to this monster, again, not by a sledge hammer but through the mobilization of every available peaceful mean; chief among them, education and enlightenment.

Fatherly admonishments to erring nations and the victimizers will have no effect and would serve no purpose. Nor would a Salvation Army approach or a Boy Scout tactic eradicate this obstinate ailment afflicting the human race. In need is a strict, yet a realistic and sensible approach to fight this scourge.

Since the past fifty years, the United Nations has been encouraging Governments and Non-Governmental Organizations to actively participate in reporting, rescuing and even rehabilitating the victims of slavery throughout the world. Former members of the Warsaw Pact countries (the former Soviet Union and its satellite countries) before 1992 paid the least attention to the dozens of resolutions passed by the United Nations through the various sub-committees of Human Rights to actively rout out this scourge. These governments were actively involved in slave labor with the victims living and dying in slave-like conditions within their own country's borders.

The majority of those countries not aligned with the Soviet bloc however showed interests to fight this menace, but no practical steps were ever taken to even curb the trade of modern-day slavery.

It was however, after the breakup of the Soviet Union and the Warsaw Pact that those same countries within the Pact now looked nervously at a growing trade of slavery within and outside their territories. They realized that the trade of slavery had increased, thanks to porous borders, unemployment and abject poverty including broken families.

As has been noted, the vastitude of slave trade in the western hemisphere is mostly from Eastern European countries where thousands of underage girls are sold into prostitution, which is virtual slavery, but on a "benign" scale. A larger scale of trade in slavery and human smuggling and trafficking in East Asia is mainly to cater to the needs of both the Arab countries as well as Western and Southern European countries.

Human beings buy, trade, auction and even barter other human beings while some governments stand by helplessly or at the most passively denounce the acts of slavery. In many cases, it is the governments who themselves indulge in slave labor by rendering punishments to "disobedient" human beings! The former Soviet Union and its satellite states in the past did it and still do it. China, The Islamic Republic of Iran,

North Korea and Cuba continuously enslaved their own people for any slight wrongdoing against the State.

Draconian measures of isolating those particular erring countries who unabatedly enslave their own people are just one of the remedies. A total socio-economic boycott of the erring country is one of those remedies. The bitter fact is that virtually all the countries in the world are involved in slavery, one way or the other.

If anything has to be done to remedy this global misery, it must be done now and that too with true vigor and determination. If this case has to be taken up by those governments who have true intentions and who are willing to rescue hundreds of millions of humans from chains, fetters and ropes, then something drastic and even revolutionary has to be done.

A new "Peaceful Manhattan Project" has to be launched! A war of liberation of mankind-by-mankind has to commence in earnest. It will be a crusade that the young and old, the strong and the feeble, the rich and the poor must all join hands in an iron bond to fight for the inalienable rights of mankind on earth; freedom.

Nationality, ethnicity, class and strata should no longer count! All must be united, all must contribute, and all must help. The mightiest tsunami of freedom must be launched immediately. The total and absolute mobilization with every ounce of resources to slay this monster of slavery by every peaceful means is the only way. Each and every country of the world; even those neutral countries having no membership with the United Nations must join hands, and join their hands now, and go forth with the war of liberation against slavery in each and every form.

If a radical change vis-à-vis the absolute freedom of humanity has to be witnessed by the world, then radical steps have to be elected and promulgated. Initially, a vow, a promise and an oath has to be taken by all the countries of the world to combat the evils of slavery and to eschew forced labors against their own people. It would only be after this vow that the particular country could be welcomed as a member-country sworn to eradicate and wipe out this ancient assault on humanity.

Signs of success in the global campaign against slavery may at first create financial limitations to those families throughout the world who depended on a paltry income flowing in from abroad through their enslaved family members, who managed to earn a small amount from their enslavers. Neither will those families who sell their daughters to unscrupulous traffickers have this opportunity any longer. Their income will stop.

A sudden stoppage to this firmly rooted disease of slavery will drastically affect individuals and families in poor countries; practically every country in the world will be affected by a sudden surge in poverty and misery, leading to more crime and chaos. After all, slavery earns criminals billions, tens of billions of U.S. dollars annually, including the family members of the slaves too, albeit a very negligible amount.

Then, of what use and value would be the much vaunted and hoped "Peaceful Manhattan Project" to smash all existing vestiges of slavery for the last time. What purpose would it serve after all, if the immediate results would be such a grand scale of misery and social instability?

Enough budget must be laid aside by participating governments to compensate the foreseeable drop in family income of the victims who have by now come to depend on money, however meager, but earned through sex-slavery and forced labor. The plan would serve many purposes if properly launched and tactically led. It would cost less than a third of the amount in comparison to the U.S. led invasion of Iraq, which cost nearly three trillion dollars! This will be a true service to humanity at large. A trillion dollars would ultimately set free a hundred million human beings and destroy the accursed disease of slavery, once and for all.

Both the traffickers and the victims must be traced and identified with billions invested in education, housing, health services and total rehabilitation.

The volunteer countries would need to unite and coordinate all efforts to take on the smugglers and the traffickers, including those who are directly and indirectly related to slavery. If the criminals refuse to halt their activities within the time of a global date set to end their trade, hand in their slaves and peacefully disband, the governments should strike against their very infrastructure.

The "Global Front for the total and absolute eradication of Slavery" thus goes into action. A World War against the evasive evil of slavery will be launched with every hope of success. The declaration is to be nationally announced by every individual country unconditionally and without any clause or hesitation.

This does not mean to prepare the members of the armed forces of participating countries to mobilize all their resources to create one giant "firing squad" to annihilate those responsible for modern-day slavery. Peaceful, yet determined volunteers outnumber the armed forces of any given country.

If there are such important calendar events as Father's Day, President's Day, Christmas, New Year's Day and many more that are meaningful, then why not add "World against Slavery Day" to the calendar year of each and every country. Once this mission is accomplished, perhaps after years of toil, only then there could be a day called "World Free of Slavery Day!"

Why not prepare the groundwork to wage a peaceful war of attrition against the "businesspeople of human flesh" before taking the sword? It is an undeniable truth that the traffickers, smugglers and slave dealers have lived a life of crime and rendered violence to other human beings, not violence, but the rules of the land should be delivered to them in case they fail to obey and disband.

There should not be any form of leniency or mercy in the weakest vein and befitting punishment should be administered immediately to those involved in this abominable trade only in case all peaceful measures fail. Nevertheless, this does not mean that the governments should erect gallows or unleash their armed forces to tear inside the flesh of these victimizers.

The results of a crushing defeat over the forces of evil; slavery, in every form and dimension conceivable will surmount humanity's greatest achievements in the past millennium. Written history will remember this event in red letters and as the greatest war waged ostensibly by humanity for the good of humankind. This war will earn the praise and gratitude of billions on earth.

Millions who are already in bondage and enslaved is one subject and those who appear to be a potential slave in the future is another topic. Both beggar equal attention. Both need immediate deliverance. There is the urgent need to liberate those who are already drawn into this web of poverty and those that may be drawn in to this web in the future by those inebriated with the love of slavery.

All said, all discussed and all argued one simple tactic to defy the trafficker, the agent, the branch of organized crime involved in slavery, is just prevention. Prevention would be arduous, a task that could only be undertaken by responsible parents and in their absence, the guardians of those growing up children. Once the correctitude of life and living is injected into these adults of tomorrow, they will confront poverty, misery and future travails in life through education, and the will to lead a normal life.

Mass media, including every available private and state-run television channels could be very instrumental and should be mobilized as participants in this "Mission of Peace" to deliver freedom to humanity.

In all honorable truth, albeit an approach of decency has no place in dealing with these cowardly victimizers of humankind, yet, logic dictates that non-violent means appear to be the most effective. One cannot always fight fire with fire in a decisive battle; water in abundance is there!

Finally, the most appropriate quote is the famous words of Nelson Mandela:

> "Education is the most powerful weapon which you can use to change the world."